Mastering

Team Leadership

---

7 Essential Coaching Skills

Mark Kelly
Robert Ferguson
George Alwon

Mark Kelly Books
Raleigh, North Carolina

Cover Design: Susan Read
Cartoons: Reprinted by permission of The Cartoon Bank

~

Book orders: Visit our website at www.RaleighConsulting.com for
current ways to order. Or try Amazon.com. For quantity discounts and special arrangements, call Mark Kelly at 800-825-
4306.

For more information about 360 feedback, executive coaching,
training, or speaking to groups, call Raleigh Consulting Group,
Inc. at 800-825-4306.

This book is dedicated to the executives, managers,
supervisors, and front line workers
who serve as team leaders.

. . . and to our family members, friends, teachers, mentors, and
coaches who helped us along the way.

. . . and especially to Dennis Coates, Ph.D.,
who laid the foundation upon which this book is built.

Contents

"*Very impressive, Mr. Crawley, but no one on our side of the table wants to feel your muscle.*"

Introduction

What is a team?

Teams are the fundamental building blocks of today's organizations. They come in many forms:
- work teams
- project teams
- cross-functional teams
- global business teams
- e-commerce teams
- virtual teams
- and many more . . .

In fact, a team is any group that works together to achieve goals, including management teams, crews, staffs, boards, and committees.

There have always been teams. The first humans who hunted saber-toothed tigers probably did so in teams. Explorers, villagers, warriors, minstrels, builders, athletes, inventors, astronauts, entrepreneurs — most human activities are done in teams.

And the team approach is here to stay. As business moves from bricks to clicks, more and more projects will depend on pooled talent and collective intelligence.

What is team leadership?

Whether as a top executive, manager, supervisor, or front line worker — team leaders of all kinds have held several important jobs:

- getting results from groups of people
- making teams more cooperative and efficient
- speeding up innovation and adaptability
- making companies more profitable

As long as organizations have tried to reach beyond the limitations of top-down management, they've needed teams and team leaders.

You would think that with so many team leaders and so much history, team leadership would be easily mastered.

Think again.

Today's team leaders face new challenges. They must guide their teams in our new downsized, reengineered, flattened, increasingly high-tech organizations. Rules are changing, chain-of-command is unclear, and the roles of virtually everyone are continually shifting.

> "We've got to run faster, jump higher, and adapt quicker than ever before."

If you are a team leader today, you will definitely encounter a variety of new situations that require mastery
of several skills:

1. *When you are the new kid on the block.* Maybe you've
    joined an existing team in the middle of an important
    project. That takes highly developed communication
    and team leadership skills.

2. *When you're asked to lead people in a new way.* You
    might be new to the team approach. If you are used
    to top-down management, skills that worked before
    can now cause problems. Coaching skills will help you
    shift to a cooperation-oriented approach.

3. *When the entire team or organization is new.* Perhaps
    you're a leader of a newly formed team, or you're
    part of a new company. Your relationship-building
    skills and problem-solving abilities are crucial.

4. *When the economy itself is new.* The new economy is
    challenging all team leaders because:
    - technology is evolving at a dizzying pace
    - geographical distances and boundaries are be-
      coming less significant
    - customers have many choices, so competitive
      pressures are growing

No matter how high-tech or global today's businesses
become, people-working-with-people is needed to deliver
results.

What is mastery?

Any organization reaching for peak performance needs its team leaders to reach for mastery.

To master any skill, a person has to make a long-term commitment to self-improvement. This is the opposite of the quick-fix mentality that characterizes many aspects of our society today.

Mastery takes daily commitment to gradual progress. It's not about perfection, it's about *practice.* Sure, there are breakthroughs at times, but mastering a skill mostly involves many small steps forward — periods where growth and change are not dramatic.

A person strives for mastery partly because it tends to bring economic rewards and a positive reputation. But deeper motives for pursuing mastery include self-respect, commitment to quality, and respect for others. Reaching mastery of any set of competencies brings enormous satisfaction and contributes to solid success.

But mastery is not for the impatient. It requires:
- practice, practice, practice
- a tenacious commitment to learning
- willingness to take risks
- one or more mentors

What is coaching?

Coaching is more than pep talks or pushing people to try harder.

Coaching is:
- mentoring others to achieve maximum results
- an investment in positive relationships
- a leadership style that fits perfectly with the team approach because it places a high value on accountability, mastery, and collaboration

Athletes and performers use coaches to reach peak performance, and most people who accomplish great things have a mentor. To master a new set of skills, we all need someone who can help us shift perspective. Someone who can provide encouragement without flattery. Someone who knows how to give constructive feedback that might be hard to hear. Someone who is an ally but not a "yes person." You can benefit by working with a coach; you can bring out the best in others by improving your own coaching skills.

Some authors have detailed hundreds of skills necessary for effective team leadership. This book focuses on seven of the most essential. They happen to be skills that executive coaches also strive to master.

Today's team leader LISTENS for success by practicing seven essential coaching skills:

Leading by example
Interactive listening
Stimulating innovation
Trusting the team
Empowered decision-making
Nurturing dialogue
Solution-focused coaching

These skills involve well-established, well-defined practices that can be learned and mastered. These skills improve team success because they
- develop a team leader who is a role model for personal commitment
- create an environment of trust and openness on the team
- increase the likelihood of making wise decisions
- help the team work smarter
- allow the team to adapt quickly to new challenges

How can you get the most from this book?

The book is designed to be practical.

First, you can use the assessment section (Appendix 1) to zero in on the parts of the book that are most relevant to you and your team.

Of course, reading the entire book is the best way to reap the greatest benefits, but if your time is very limited or you learn best by following your curiosity, start reading anywhere. You might choose to concentrate on the chapters most relevant to you. Each chapter offers pragmatic value on its own.

Then, work with an executive coach or personal coach as you put these principles into practice.

Carefully read the dialogues between team leaders and their coaches. Look for the types of problems and challenges you face. The details vary from company to company, but all leaders face similar people issues. We created these conversations to show how coaches help leaders improve and excel. The dialogues were inspired by our many years of collective experience in consulting, psychology, coaching, and 360 feedback.

If you have been involved in a 360 feedback process, use this book to study and master communication and leadership skills that your 360 revealed as a concern. If you are unfamiliar with 360 feedback, see Appendix 3 for an overview.

Finally, consider sharing the book with your team. You work as a team, why not learn as a team?

Chapter 1

LEADING BY EXAMPLE

"Ok honesty is the best policy.
Let's call that option A."

What is leading by example?

As a team leader, others constantly observe you.

That makes you a role model, whether you like it or not.

Leading by example involves using your status as role model very deliberately. How you actually approach the many changes and challenges a team faces — decisions, problems, time pressures, disagreements, new members, etc. — has more impact on team members' attitudes and performance than do your words.

Leading by example is your most powerful tool for inspiring others to reach for excellence. It means you do what you say you will do. It means you conduct yourself with the highest degree of personal integrity. It means you act as you expect others to act. Leading by example is the strongest way for a leader to inspire others to do their best.

Why is leading by example so important?

If leaders want team members to care about their work, to open up to new ideas, and to commit to team goals, the leader must act as a living example of these qualities.

Team members will believe actions over words. A leader may claim a certain standard is important, but if the leader's actions contradict such a statement, team members will discount what was said and follow the leader's actions.

People want and need leaders who live by high ethical standards. When you lead by example, you usually find a receptive and motivated group of team members who are willing to cooperate. Leaders who do not practice what they preach eventually find a group of cynical followers who resist progress.

> "Walk your talk."

◈ PROFILE OF A SUCCESSFUL TEAM LEADER

Ten tips for leading by example:

1. **Contribute important skills and abilities to the total team effort.** While you may have important technical skills, your leadership and management skills are more instrumental in assisting the team and the organization.

2. **Improve your knowledge and skills.** When you stop learning, your ability to contribute declines. You invest in your team when you demonstrate your curiosity with an open mind and a willingness to experiment.

3. **Enhance your relationships skills and increase positive thinking.** You influence others when you illustrate these interrelated abilities:
    - maintaining personal health
    - demonstrating a "can-do" attitude
    - persisting in the face of daily problems and setbacks
    - accepting responsibility for your mistakes (this is not the same as self-blame or guilt)
    - following through on promises
    - showing sensitivity for people
    - remaining calm in high-pressure situations

4. **Maintain a customer focus and insist on quality.** Quality is defined by what matters most to your customers. If you are unable or unwilling to do what is

necessary to fulfill their expectations for quality, customers will look elsewhere.

5. **Manage your time.** You create a ripple effect when you organize your tasks so that high-priority actions come first. Your example is contagious for the entire team.

6. **Take initiative.** You must be willing to take initiative, bring matters to the attention of the right people and then empower them to act.

7. **Demonstrate high standards of ethical conduct.** People need to know they can trust their leaders to do what is right, tell the truth and uphold a high level of personal integrity. It is the foundation for mutual respect.

8. **Deal fairly with people.** You don't have to treat everyone exactly the same in order to be fair. When opportunities arise for interesting assignments or promotions, team members expect the leader to deal with them in an impartial way. Easy to say, hard to do.

9. **Protect information considered by the team to be personal or confidential.** The failure to protect private matters can be embarrassing and hurtful. To build enduring trust among the team, it is important to create a climate where confidential issues can be discussed without fear of disclosure.

10. **Ask for support.** As a team leader, when you ask for appropriate support, you are not only more likely to succeed at the specific task, you are a role model for cooperation.

> "Act as you expect others to act."

⊙ DIALOGUE WITH AN EXECUTIVE COACH

"Houston, we have a problem."

Brian is general manager of the technical division of a global biotechnology firm. He is trying to build business teams within the division to bring about better customer focus and closer coordination between various locations around the world. He is a leader with a vision, and is concerned his teams are not maturing fast enough.

Brian: Mark, good to see you again. I'm sorry I kept you waiting. I was on the phone with my ten-year-old son. He's all excited about some movie he wants me to rent.

Coach: Which one?

Brian: We watched *Raiders of the Lost Ark* last night. Now he wants to watch all the Indiana Jones movies.

Coach: Great flicks! They remind me of a great comic book.

Brian: With lots of action. My son and I both love the action scenes. If only I could get my business teams to look more like an action movie. That's why I wanted to talk to you today.

Coach: What's the matter?

Brian: Everything is going too slow — the team-building process, the teams working together, progress toward goals — it's all too slow. I'm wondering if there's any-thing I need to be doing differently to accelerate things.

Coach: Tell me about the situation.

Brian: I handpicked these teams. Best people in the company. I thought I was reaching for the moon. Now I feel like I'm just trying to stay alive.

Coach: What's the objective of these teams?

Brian: Each team needs to take ownership of their cus-tomer base and their identified market. They need to coordinate their efforts and focus on hitting their team goals. And they need to do it *together*.

Coach: "Take ownership"? I'm not sure I know what you mean.

Brian: I mean they need to feel responsible — like I do. They need to be accountable for their goals and deci-sions, the way I have to be. And I want them to follow through when they make a commitment to get things done.

Coach: So what is it you want to change or improve?

Brian: I just told you.

Coach: Well, I heard what you want the *teams* to do better. But I'm asking if you know what *you* want to do differently in terms of leadership style.

Brian: I'm not sure we're on the same page here, Mark. I'm in charge of building these teams, and I need to speed up the process. I want some strategies.

Coach: So part of your concern is the teams' basic performance, how they're coming together. And your other concern is about wanting things to develop at a quicker pace. Is that it?

Brian: I'd say that's basically it.

Coach: And you want to focus on what *you* could do differently?

Brian: Right.

Coach: Okay, tell me what you've done so far.

Brian: I've set up a steering committee and the seven business teams. I've eliminated several middle managers who were slowing things down. But whatever I do, the pace doesn't seem to pick up.

Coach: What do you see as the main obstacles?

Brian: I'm not sure. It might be a lack of confidence on the part of the team leaders. That's frustrating since I handpicked this group. I thought I chose people who were willing to speak their mind, but they just seem to go along with whatever I say.

I can't get people to challenge me. They back down whenever I disagree with what they're proposing. They know I like a good debate. They know I like to be challenged as much as I like to challenge others. That's how people and organizations improve.

Coach: So now you're wondering if you misjudged some of these team leaders.

Brian: It's possible. But I'm also thinking they need more training on how teams work. Or maybe the problem has more to do with how the teams are structured. That's why I need your input.

Coach: Slow team development is usually not about team structure or training. It's usually more about management style and how the leader isn't transferring ownership to the teams.

Brian: Mark, wait. Let's stay focused. I *want* them to take ownership. The problem is they won't do it. I'm trying to transfer decisions and leadership, and all I'm seeing is passivity and resistance.

Coach: Are you sure you want to focus on what *you* can do differently?

Brian: Yes — what I can do differently to speed up the teams . . .

Coach: And so far you've made decisions with that goal in mind. Even some of the major team decisions you've made are aimed at speeding things up.

Brian: Yes, I believe time is crucial in this economy. That guides many of my major decisions.

Coach: To the point you sometimes feel it's necessary to override your team leaders' decisions. You think some of their decisions will result in slowing things down, so you step in and redirect things.

Brian: Exactly. I have to.

Coach: And sometimes you even have to remove people from leadership positions because you see them as contributing to the slower pace.

Brian: Right.

Coach: What do you see as the consequences of the approach you're currently taking to speed things up?

Brian: Mark, I'm not sure you're listening. There are no consequences. I'm admitting it's not working.

Coach: But I thought you said all you see is resistance.

Brian: That's what I mean. Nothing's happening.

Coach: What I'm getting at, Brian, is that there's another way of looking at this. Maybe the resistance you see *is* what's happening. And you're helping to create it.

Brian: Mark, I think we're getting off on the wrong foot here. What I liked about our first session was your apparent emphasis on taking responsibility. Half the problems in the world today are a result of someone blaming someone else instead of taking responsibility for their actions.

Coach: I'm saying there's a possibility you are not taking full responsibility for your actions in this situation.

Brian: Look, let's stop right here. I don't like the way this is going.

Coach: Hang in here with me, Brian. Part of my job as coach is to tell you things other people aren't willing to tell you. You said you like to be challenged. I'm challenging you.

Brian: I like my *ideas* to be challenged.

Coach: And I'm challenging the idea that you expect your teams to take ownership of their decisions if you're still making the major decisions. Every time you override a decision — and certainly when you remove one of the players — you're sending a vote of "no confidence."

Brian: If what you're saying is true, why aren't people telling me?

Coach: They *are* telling you. They're just not being as clear as I am. They've got more to lose. I could see how people might want to be pretty cautious around you and keep their heads low. Their resistance might be an understated way of saying they don't trust you. Here, let me put it another way. Have you ever seen the movie *Apollo 13*?

Brian: Yes. I rented it a few months ago with my son. What about it?

Coach: Who's the hero of that movie?

Brian: The main guy. The astronaut, Tom Hanks.

Coach: No. Think about it. He would have been dead if it weren't for the guys on the ground. The engineers and mission controllers back in Houston and Florida kept solving problems, and making decisions, and thinking up ways to get the ship back in one piece.

Brian: Yeah, I remember. Okay, I see where we're going. The hero of the movie is the team.

Coach: Right. Everybody in the film — especially the leaders — believes in the team. Which character did you like the best?

Brian: That one guy . . . what's his name? The guy in charge back in Houston. The one who says, "Failure is not an option!" I love that line. That's how I live.

Coach: Every time a new problem came up, he kept telling the team to come up with a solution.

Brian: I remember that.

Coach: Well, that's team leadership. He was leading by example. He was saying over and over again that the team has the ability to get the job done.

Brian: That's how he builds confidence.

Coach: Yep. And that's how he *wins* confidence.

Brian: Okay, I see your point. So how can a strong-minded manager like me build teams faster?

Coach: What's your role on the steering committee?

Brian: I'm the chairman. When we set this up, our consultants said it was important to show my commitment by leading the way. So I chair every meeting, just like I'm supposed to.

Coach: Maybe you could change your role to sponsor, and remove yourself from the steering committee, but have team leaders keep you informed of team decisions and progress. What effect do you think that might have?

Brian: It would show I trust their decision-making ability. But I'd be nervous they might make decisions about issues that aren't within their scope of authority.

Coach: That makes sense. What could you do to build in a safeguard without undercutting their confidence? What kind of boundaries could you set?

Brian: Uh . . . we could clearly define what decisions are within the steering committee's scope and what decisions I feel I need to reserve. But I want to do more than remove myself as an obstacle by getting out of the room. I want them to open up in front of me — challenge me if they think I'm wrong.

Coach: If you give them permission to disagree with you, be sure not to kill the messenger when you don't like what you hear. You said you got rid of several people who were slowing things down.

Brian: It wasn't because they disagreed with me. But I can see how the others might get that message.

Coach: You reacted pretty strongly when I first challenged you. I imagine you've done that in team meetings. It could take a while to repair the trust between you and the team leaders. What could you do about that?

Brian: First, I could be more open to challenges like yours. I probably take some challenges too personally. Second, I better tell them why I'm getting off the steering committee and then listen to what they have to say about that.

Coach: Those are good ideas. How will you know if this new approach is working?

Brian: Well, I hope I'll see things speeding up. But I'm going to remember *Apollo 13* and try to be patient. I guess I'll watch for more participation and honesty.

Coach: Good.

Brian: And I'm going to be less like Indiana Jones and more like mission control.

Coach: Roger that, Houston. I think we're back on track.

☑ PERSONAL DEVELOPMENT SUGGESTIONS

Take an inventory of your strengths and contributions to the team. Ask your manager and coworkers to list your three most important contributions to the team. Then ask what you can do to add more value to the total team effort.

Identify some specific goals for improving your contribution. Choose one or two specific areas you want to focus on improving. Write them down as specifically as you can. For example: "I will improve my ability to follow through on my commitments by writing down all the promises I make in my day planner and checking them every morning."

Learn something new from a member of your team. Identify some new skill you need to learn and one of your team members who could tutor you. Be a willing and eager learner. This sends a powerful message about respect for team members, continuous learning and teamwork. Encourage others on the team to "buddy up" and teach each other something. Cross-pollinate.

Use this book as a personal development tool. Take one chapter a week. Spend 15 minutes reading through it at the beginning of the week. Pick one item a day to focus on. Jot notes to yourself as you find yourself applying each tip or as you notice others doing so. Each week, have a different team member be your "spotter" and point out when you need to get back on track.

To gain insight, ask yourself these questions:

- What example will I be setting with my current behavior? How would I want another team member to
  handle this situation?

- What have I done lately to learn something new, try
  something different or make a change to improve my
  effectiveness? What has my team done lately to
  learn?

**Practice a mindset that will help you lead by exam-
ple:**

- *"I am a role model."*

- *"My actions speak louder than my words."*

- *"I am accountable for my actions."*

Chapter 2

INTERACTIVE LISTENING

"So, does anyone in the group feel like responding
to what Richard has just shared with us?"

What is interactive listening?

Interactive listening is "listening with" someone instead of just "listening to" them. It means to interact with the speaker in such a way that it is clear you are fully engaged and focused on understanding what the speaker is trying to communicate.

Interactive listening requires you to suspend judgment temporarily as to the "rightness" of the speaker's message. Instead, your energy is focused on taking in as much meaning from the speaker as possible. The goal is to understand the message as completely as possible, not to decide whether you agree or disagree.

Why is interactive listening so important?

How you listen is fundamental in the development of all of your work relationships. How the listener behaves is the single most important factor in determining the quantity and quality of all future feedback.

Interactive listening is the vehicle for team leaders to establish an environment of trust and openness on the team. Helping people express their perspectives clearly and completely is necessary for the team leader to get full contribution from all team members.

Leaders spend more time communicating than doing anything else. If they are smart, they listen — and listen well. They listen to their team members, their customers, their managers, and their suppliers.

Leaders should have the goal of finding out what is in people's heads. They listen so they can anticipate problems and get the information they need to solve them.

The team-building process happens at both the individual level and the team level. The team leader needs to take the time to develop trust with each member of the team, as well as to actively promote openness among team members. And the process begins with interactive listening.

> "I know you believe you understood what you think I said, but I'm not sure you realize that what you heard is not what I meant."

◈ PROFILE OF A SUCCESSFUL TEAM LEADER

Ten tips for interactive listening:

1. **Invite contact.** Team members have a lot of valuable information to share with their leaders about project status, customer concerns, emerging problems and more. Good team leaders are easy to approach and easy to talk to.

2. **Give your full attention to the speaker.** When someone is talking to you, giving the person your full attention sends the message that you value the person *and* the message. Good team leaders discipline themselves to stop what they are doing and focus 100% of their attention on understanding what the other person is saying.

3. **Show a genuine interest.** When you let people know you are sincerely interested in what they have to say, they will give you more information. Communication will be easier and smoother. People will find the experience more satisfying. Trust will continue to build.

4. **Listen to others . . .**
   - **without interrupting.** Some people struggle to express themselves clearly. Interrupting someone who is already having trouble getting their message across can disrupt their thought process and their openness to communicate further. Hold your own thoughts until you have heard you team member's complete message.

- **without changing the subject.** We all have a lot on our minds. But changing the subject sends a powerful message that what the other person has to say is not important.
- **without finding fault.** One of the worst times to find fault is when someone is trying to communicate something. Effective team leaders know that people need to feel comfortable if they are going to talk about problems and concerns freely — without being blamed for bringing the issues to light.

5. **Maintain appropriate eye contact with the speaker.** Appropriate eye contact does not mean an intense, hard stare. It is simply a friendly, interested look to let the speaker know you are paying attention.

6. **Encourage the speaker to continue talking to get more information.** People do not normally talk in complete, well-polished thoughts. Usually they begin with the part that interests them most and then they expand their thoughts into relevant side issues. Effective leaders ask questions to help the speaker "flesh out" the message.

7. **Notice the speaker's tone of voice, gestures and facial expressions.** There is no one-to-one code for nonverbal messages. Smart leaders pay attention to nonverbal aspects of communication so they can better interpret how others feel. This involves seeing all nonverbal signals as a coordinated message.

8. **Ask questions to check understanding.** Even careful listeners frequently misunderstand some aspect of what a speaker is trying to say. The easiest way to make sure you "got it" is simply to ask some clarification questions. It also lets the speaker know you are fully engaged.

9. **Summarize the speaker's thoughts, feelings and ideas.** Sometimes a speaker's message is somewhat disorganized. You can help by restating in your own words what you think the speaker is trying to tell you. Pay attention not only to the words but also to the underlying feeling behind the words. The speaker can then verify that you understood or try new words to make the message clearer.

10. **Receive constructive feedback without getting defensive.** Feedback is information given to people about behavior or performance. Wise leaders view constructive feedback as a gift that helps them enhance their own effectiveness. Wise leaders learn how not to act defensively even when the feedback is unpleasant. They value accurate, uncensored assessment.

⊙ DIALOGUE WITH AN EXECUTIVE COACH

"It's never too late for good leadership."

Beverly is the new team leader in the accounting department of an insurance services company. After only six months in her new position, she is preparing to fire one of her team members. The employee is capable but is not performing up to Beverly's expectations.

Beverly is now trying to analyze how things got to this point. She has hired an executive coach to help her further develop effective leadership skills. She talks to her coach once a month by telephone.

Beverly: Hi, George. I'm so glad we have a session scheduled today.

Coach: What's up? You sound a little tense.

Beverly: Well, I have to fire one of my employees tomorrow, and I'm feeling nervous about it. I haven't had to let someone go for a long time, and I'm remembering how much I hate this part of the job.

Coach: Most managers say the same thing; it can be pretty unpleasant. You sound like your mind isn't quite made up, though. Are you questioning whether you're doing the right thing?

Beverly: No. I'm convinced this is the right thing to do. But I'm frustrated because I hired this guy about a year ago. His credentials were good, his work experience was solid, and he was very articulate about technological changes in the insurance industry. He made a good impression with everyone who interviewed him.

Coach: He sounds pretty sharp.

Beverly: That's why I'm so surprised. For the first two or three months he was doing okay. But then he started making mistakes, and it's been getting worse over the last several months. It's to the point where I feel I have no choice but to let him go.

Coach: What kind of mistakes are you talking about?

Beverly: Well, he's responsible for accounts receivable. And he's making mistakes like leaving out department numbers and not balancing up the accounts exactly.

Coach: Beverly, those don't sound like fatal mistakes. Could it be time for another meeting of Perfectionists Anonymous?

Beverly: (*She laughs.*) George, I know I have those tendencies; that's one of the reasons I hired you. But this is a different issue, really. Charlie's job requires good attention to detail and he knows that. And it's not just a few mistakes; it's a string of them. They make us look sloppy to our customers and suppliers, and I don't want to have to always look over his shoulder to make sure all the "i's" are dotted and the "t's" are crossed.

Coach: You said you're frustrated. You also sound embarrassed.

Beverly: Embarrassed? I guess I am. I'm the one who hired him. I'm responsible for the quality of work that goes out of here. It makes me look so unprofessional! And it's a reflection on the whole department.

Coach: You sound angry, too.

Beverly: I guess I am getting a bit worked up. The thing is, I know this guy is capable of doing the work because he did it well for the first couple of months. It's like he just doesn't care any more.

Coach: Have you talked to him about it?

Beverly: Several times. I had an informal talk with him about three months ago and another talk about a month ago where I was fairly strong in saying some things needed to improve. I didn't come out and say his job was on the line, but I'm pretty sure he got the message.

Coach: How did he respond?

Beverly: He didn't say much either time. In both cases he was pretty quiet, and both times he sent an email that sort of acknowledged he could do better and saying he would work on improving. The thing is, George, I don't think he really means it.

But I didn't give up easy. I figured he was more comfortable with email, so I sent him a list of the mistakes he made and tried to give him a clear picture of what I'm talking about.

Coach: Hang on a second, Beverly. I'm getting confused. On the one hand, you say you talked to him about this twice and that you made yourself clear. On the other hand, you say you didn't exactly come out and tell him his job was at stake. You also say he hasn't said much when you talk but you can tell he's getting the message. And now the two of you are mostly using email to communicate? It doesn't sound like you have really connected with him yet.

Beverly: Well, when you put it that way, maybe we haven't really communicated. But it's not for lack of trying on my part. Besides, it's gone on too long, and my boss is starting to ask questions about him. Charlie is acting like he's not a member of the team. As the team leader, I have to take action. My mind is made up.

Coach: You sound defensive.

Beverly: I guess I do. I feel like I'm defending my decision with you, as if you think this is about my perfectionism rather than the quality of his work.

Coach: I shouldn't have joked about that before. I'm sorry about that.

Beverly: This guy's really messing up, George.

Coach: I believe you. I really do. And I want you to know that I'm not focusing here on the quality of his work. That's not my job in this situation. My job is to help you master your skills as a team leader so you can be as successful as possible.

Beverly: That's what I want — peak performance.

Coach: I know.

Beverly: Okay, so what does this have to do with my skills?

Coach: Well, you say you've done everything you could. Apparently you believe the situation is all his responsibility. But I think you have some responsibility here, too.

Beverly: You're back to saying this is my fault.

Coach: I didn't use the word "fault," Beverly. I said "responsibility." As in "ability-to-respond." I'm saying there may be some other ways you could respond to him that would, in turn, produce different responses from him.

Beverly: But what else can I do, George? I've talked to him twice. I've clarified my expectations. I pointed out very specifically the types of mistakes he's making. And I thought I was doing him a favor by keeping it informal, so his record wouldn't look bad. I really feel like it's too late to give him any more chances.

Coach: That may be. But it's never too late for good leadership. And it's not too late to use this situation to learn about how to improve *your* team leadership.

Beverly: I like that idea. If there's a mistake I'm making here — if I have some "blind spot" as you like to call it — this could happen again.

Coach: So if you're going to fire him, maybe you can have an extended exit interview and let him tell you why he thinks it came to this. We haven't really heard from him yet. Since he has nothing to lose, if you ask the right questions and listen without debating what he has to say — even if you disagree with it — you might get some valuable information.

Beverly: What kind of questions would you suggest?

Coach: I'd rather you tell me. Think about it. What do you want to know?

Beverly: Well, I want to know why the quality of his work kept slipping. I want to know why he wouldn't talk about it to me, and why we seemed to communicate more by email than face-to-face lately. And I guess I want to know if there's anything I've done to contribute to this. But that's asking a lot, considering his behavior so far. Do you think he'd really tell me?

Coach: Maybe. It probably depends mostly on how you listen and respond to his answers.

Beverly: Okay, let me think. I could ask something like, "What were you thinking when you read my email detailing your mistakes?" and "Are there ways I've communicated with you that made this situation worse?"

Coach: Those are good. Also, I'd recommend that instead of trying to discuss his answers, just summarize and reflect back to him what he says. That will let him know you really heard him.

Beverly: I think I'm getting this. It's like being a mirror. I'm reflecting instead of *reacting* to him.

Coach: That's it exactly. And it might give him the room to say what he really thinks rather than simply trying to avoid you.

Beverly: Okay. This makes sense.

Coach: And since we're not scheduled to talk for another month, why don't you give me a quick call in a few days just to tell me how things went.

Beverly: I'd like that. It's a good idea.

(*Follow-up phone call two days later . . .*)

Coach: Hi, Beverly. How did it go with Charlie?

Beverly: Very well. Better than I could have possibly hoped for. The first words out of his mouth were about finding another opportunity, and he said he was moving on in two weeks. I was stunned. I had my opening lines all memorized and had to trash them.

Coach: Then what happened?

Beverly: I just sat there for about thirty seconds collecting my thoughts. Then I realized I could still ask him the questions I'd written down. So I started with, "What caused you to come to this decision?"

Coach: Could you summarize the conversation for me?

Beverly: Sure. In fact, that would be good practice. His perspective went something like this. When he was hired, he was led to believe he would have a lot of autonomy in the job. And for the first several months that was the case. He remembers me being tied up with a big project for corporate, which is true.

After that, though, he remembers a time when he made a small mistake and I came down on him pretty hard. I don't see it that way, but I kept thinking of being a mirror so I didn't react to his perception of that incident.

He said he had been hurt by how I handled that early mistake, and he concluded I didn't have confidence in him. Then, when he made another mistake, he just kind of gave up because it seemed like the more he tried, the more I looked over his shoulder trying to catch him. He used the word "hover." That stung, but I kept listening and reflecting.

Coach: It can be difficult.

Beverly: He said that after a while he starting losing confidence in himself. He realized how important having more autonomy was to him. So he is going to set up his own bookkeeping business for several small companies in the area.

Coach: Good for him, and good for you. What did you learn from this?

Beverly: Well, I couldn't resist asking him if he thought I was a perfectionist. He kind of smiled, and that's when he used the word "hover."

And since he's not the only person who makes comments about my perfectionist tendencies, I've learned it's an area I need to pay attention to. I tell people I want them to take responsibility — and I mean it — but if I'm also hovering, I'm sending a mixed message.

Coach: Is there anything you could have done differently to change how this all came out?

Beverly: That's what I was thinking about last night. If I had handled that first meeting six months ago differently, maybe this whole thing would have turned out differently. I still don't agree with some of the way he sees things, but I realize that's not the point.

Now I realize that how a leader is perceived is as important as the leader's intentions. So I'll be more interactive in my listening, especially when I'm working with a new team member. I want people to know I have confidence in them. I want to work through mistakes early.

I also think I waited too long before getting involved with what he was doing. It's true I was busy with another project, but that's no excuse. I was leaving him alone and when I finally *did* get involved, it was in the wrong way. I just never realized how sensitive he was to the confidence issue.

So, I guess I had more "response-ability" for this situation than I was willing to admit two days ago. I honestly believed this was 95% his issue and 5% mine.

Coach: And now?

Beverly: I'd have to say it is at least 50-50, or maybe even a little more of my issue than his.

Coach: What made you change your mind?

Beverly: About halfway through the conversation, I actually started to understand the situation from his point of view, and it made sense to me. That's when I could see my role in contributing to the problems.

Coach: What happens now?

Beverly: I asked him if he would reconsider his decision, but he said it was too late. He had already made commitments and was excited about his new business. He actually thanked me for hearing him out and said it was the best two hours he'd had with any manager.

Coach: I imagine that was nice to hear.

Beverly: Yes, it was. I need to remember all of this the next time around.

Coach: Makes sense. Keep me posted.

☑ PERSONAL DEVELOPMENT SUGGESTIONS

Be present. When someone is trying to tell you something, stop all activity and focus 100% of your attention on that individual. Maintain eye contact, and let the person know you are listening. An occasional nod or short comments like "I see what you mean" can help illustrate your interest.

Jot down notes to yourself. As others are talking, jot down key reactions or questions that occur to you. This allows the speaker to finish without your interrupting, changing the subject, finding fault or reacting with an emotional outburst.

Before responding, reflect and ask questions. Make it a habit to summarize what the speaker has just said. Then ask a question or two and encourage the speaker to elaborate. You'll notice how much more information you can get and how much more receptive the speaker is to your response.

Solicit more feedback — and accept it gratefully. When it comes to feedback, the more you ask for, the more you'll get. Appreciate the fact that most people don't give feedback very well — whether it's a compliment or constructive criticism. Team members may believe they are taking a big risk by giving you honest feedback. It is your job to make it as safe and comfortable as possible. At a minimum, thank them with comments like "I appreciate your honesty."

Study someone else who has a reputation for being open to contact. Initiate a conversation with such a person, then pay attention to what they do that makes it easy to deal with them. What facial expressions, actions, body language or tone of voice do they use to signal they want to spend time talking to you?

To gain insight, ask yourself these questions:

- Do I have a reputation as a willing listener? Do I let people "get things off their chest" without criticizing or immediately trying to solve the problem for them?

- Am I easy to approach? What signals do I send to show I'm listening? Do I invite or solicit contact? How?

Practice a mindset that will help you master interactive listening:

- *"People who share information with me deserve to be heard."*

- *"I don't shoot the messenger."*

- *"Feedback is information gold."*

- *"I make it comfortable for people to approach and talk to me."*

"Interactive listening requires you to suspend judgment temporarily."

Chapter 3

STIMULATING INNOVATION

"Where are you going with this, Wingate?"

What is stimulating innovation?

Stimulating innovation means helping the team approach its job in new and improved ways.

It involves:
- predicting customer needs and desires
- anticipating what is happening in the business environment
- envisioning various future scenarios
- reacting to unexpected situations
- adjusting to new requirements
- discovering breakthroughs
- finding ways to improve continuously
- solving problems that have never been solved before

To cope and adapt to a changing workplace, leaders must regularly encourage people to offer fresh ideas and take risks. Beyond that, good ideas must be supported and implemented.

Why is stimulating innovation so important?

Today it is impossible to find an organization that has not been significantly influenced by change. Every aspect of the business environment is currently changing — costs, regulations, technology, customer expectations, competition and employee capabilities.

Because team members work closely with customers and products, they have a wealth of knowledge and experience that can be tapped into and utilized. And if team members are involved in the process of creating new approaches that will affect them, their support for change will be more complete.

> "Kill a new idea, and you're killing its descendants as well."

◈ PROFILE OF A SUCCESSFUL TEAM LEADER

Ten tips for stimulating innovation:

1. **Express a vision of the future.** Teams need a worthy challenge, an important reason for being. Leaders should be a strong advocate for the team *and* the organization's vision. This focus will produce the drive for improvement and innovation. It sets the stage for the team to figure out how to achieve the vision in creative ways.

2. **Encourage team members to ask "why" and to question the status quo.** Many people are uncomfortable with change. Leaders must encourage uncomfortable questions that challenge the status quo. They must show a willingness to break old habits and to show support for others who do the same.

3. **Encourage people to think creatively.** Creativity involves new associations of existing thoughts and ideas. This is not a common mode of thinking, and leaders have to ask for creative ideas on a regular basis. When people offer new ideas, they risk criticism or opposition. Smart leaders make sure new ideas are received without instant criticism.

4. **Ask team members for ideas and suggestions.** If you are serious about soliciting ideas, you need to make the process easy and satisfying. People have to believe their input is really wanted and will receive serious consideration. That means asking for sugges-

tions, giving them balanced evaluation and ensuring that the right people are involved.

5. **Suspend criticism until ideas have been heard and explored.** Research shows that teams that feel free to offer all sorts of ideas generate significantly more good suggestions than teams that try to submit *only* good ideas. It is important to separate generating ideas from judging ideas. Do not let brainstorming degenerate into a debate about the pros and cons of any one idea.

6. **Affirm the positive aspects of suggestions before stating concerns.** Constructive feedback involves a balance of both positive points and potential concerns. By affirming the positive points *first*, team leaders are acknowledging and encouraging members to keep suggesting. It also prevents killing off good ideas too early.

7. **Commit time and resources to support promising new ideas.** To survive, a good idea needs to be supported in many ways. Time must be given for people to work on it. Tools, equipment and materials must be committed for its development. It also needs intangible support like creative input and encouragement. Team leaders must combine good judgment with imagination to decide when and how to support a potentially promising idea.

8. **React constructively to challenges and setbacks.** Experienced leaders expect problems and obstacles

to arise in the face of innovation. The key is how quickly people react to problems and get on with finding solutions. Team leaders need to help the members understand the problems and obstacles, devise ways to overcome them, and do so in a way that keeps the team focused on the task at hand in a constructive frame of mind.

9. **Give praise or recognition to team members who work on innovative projects.** It is difficult to work on a project with an uncertain outcome and unexpected obstacles along the way. People who take the risk and invest the energy to tackle them need to feel rewarded for their effort. Team leaders need to recognize *everyone* who contributes — people who suggest ideas, people who devote their time, as well as the "champions" who bring the idea to fulfillment.

10. **Never kill a new idea.** The initial value of an idea is not how well it will ultimately work, but how much it supports continued creative thinking. Value every idea in its germinal form. Very often a creative but impractical idea eventually leads to a new product or procedure that is extremely pragmatic and profitable. If you kill a new idea, you're killing its descendants as well.

⊙ DIALOGUE WITH AN EXECUTIVE COACH

"Fear is not the best way to stimulate innovation."

Kramer is a product manager in a successful mid-size toy company. He reports to the president and has "dotted line" responsibilities to the vice presidents of marketing and manufacturing. The president recently assigned Kramer to implement a new product development process, which includes both marketing and manufacturing functions.

Kramer is now having trouble getting the team leaders in both departments to assist in the development of a new product line and in a new way of producing and delivering the new products.

Coach: Good morning, Kramer. Would you close the door, please?

Kramer: Listen, you've got to help me, Mark. I've got a big problem.

Coach: What's up?

Kramer: I feel like I'm in a vice-grip with both vice presidents. And the president is squeezing me even harder. Help me figure out how to relieve the pressure and get my project back on track.

Coach: Hmmm. Sounds pretty tough. Tell me more about the situation.

Kramer: It all started about two months ago. The president went to this seminar on how to be a world-class competitor. When he came back, he started talking about how we are going to have to change the way we do business.

Nobody paid much attention to him, because it sounded like motherhood and apple pie. Besides, he goes to these seminars about once a year and comes back all jazzed up. But usually nothing much happens, and he settles down in a few weeks. We all thought he was doing his annual cheerleading exercise.

But not this time! He called me into his office about a month ago and says to me, "It's time to start the change process with a new product!" Then he pulls out a blank sheet of paper and puts it on the table and says, "I want us to start by completely opening our minds as if they were like this blank piece of paper. I want you and your people to completely redesign a new product line from scratch, and I want you to come up with a completely new way of getting new products to customers!"

Coach: That's bold.

Kramer: Yeah! It's bold all right! He wants me to act as "internal champion" of this new product line and this new approach.

Coach: Sounds like he really believes in you.

Kramer: Not so fast, Mark. Because two seconds later he picks up a pen and proceeds to fill in the blank sheet of paper with *his* thoughts about how to go about it.

Coach: Oh.

Kramer: Yeah. The president is a visionary. No doubt about that. But sometimes I think he's too visionary. He was talking about completely overhauling virtually every department in the company. His enthusiasm was infectious. I could see the benefits if we could really make it happen.

But I'm skeptical we can pull it off. The manufacturing VP is a hardnosed "prove-it-to-me-first" kind of guy. And the marketing VP thinks if she and her gang of marketing people didn't think it up, it probably isn't worth considering.

Coach: Have you talked to them yet?

Kramer: Sure, I talked to both of them and about five of their people. I tried to make them understand what the president had in mind.

Coach: What kind of responses did you get?

Kramer: A lot of silence, a few questions, and a bunch of mumbles like, "Totally impossible," and "Good luck." You know, the usual "blah, blah, blah."

Coach: What did the manufacturing VP say?

Kramer: Randy made his usual speech about the negative impact on short-term efficiency and delivery dates.

Coach: How about the marketing VP?

Kramer: About what I expected. Elaine launched into a meaningless monologue about the customer as our reason for being, the need for meticulous customer research, and some fairly blunt warnings about staying out of her territory.

In the meantime, the president is asking if all is going well. I'm dodging him as best I can until I've got something good to tell him. What am I going to do?

Coach: Let's go back and analyze this. First, I wonder what your objectives are in this situation. What do you really want? You don't sound committed to the president's vision of how to change things. I get the impression you're acting like a spear-carrier for a chief who's getting shot by his own tribe.

Kramer: Ouch! Bull's eye.

Coach: Tell me a little about the new product you're working on and how you personally feel about it.

Kramer: Well, okay, but you're going to have to keep this confidential. As you know, our product line of high-tech toys is losing market share. The kids have too many choices these days. The web is making this end of our business too competitive.

So the president has this big idea to go directly after the *parents* as the market — especially stressed-out parents of *young* children. You know, the potty-training market. He's correctly pointed out that there has been no new innovation in this area since the invention of the plastic training pants.

He wants me to work with our engineers to come up with what he's already calling the Mobile Electronic Sensor System, or M.E.S.S. for short.

He wants us to develop a miniature port-o-pot on wheels that follows a homing device strapped to the busy little toddler-in-training. It would maintain a safe distance of approximately two feet from the child until sensors detect the slightest increase in the room's humidity. Within two seconds it would bump gently into the kid's legs, nudging the little one into the potty position. A recorded voice would then broadcast a verbal reward, *"You did it, sweetheart!"* And he was adamant about customizing the product; the recorded voice would be that of the child's actual mother.

Coach: What do you think about his idea?

Kramer: He sure is thinking "outside the box." But it gets even farther out of the box from here.

Coach: How so?

Kramer: He wants to run the operation strictly as an e-business. He wants to create a series of commercials showing busy two-career couples completely exhausted from trying to balance work and family. They'll look so tired at the end of their day that they can't stand to think about potty-training. But they'll look happy and relaxed when they hear about our new web site, www.ePotty.com. We'll take all orders over the web and through an 800 number.

Coach: Ambitious.

Kramer: Wait, there's more. When parents call in, they can customize their purchase by leaving a voice re-cording of their enthusiastic support for the kid's ef-forts, and then we put the whole thing together and ship within two business days. This is going to put a real strain on the customer service department as well as the folks in manufacturing.

Coach: Okay, so let's go back to what you want out of all this. Assuming the company can pull this off, what do you hope to achieve? How do you feel about being the "point-man" and "lightning rod" for making a change of this magnitude?

Kramer: We'd achieve market dominance — there's sim-ply nobody out there offering a product like this. I'd be the hottest product manager in the company — maybe the hottest in the whole industry. On the other hand, if

I'm going to be the hottest product manager, I'd better get used to a few lightning bolts.

Coach: So you see this project as potentially helping your career, but creating a lot of stress.

Kramer: If it doesn't work, it could hurt the company and my career.

Coach: What stage of the project are you in now?

Kramer: We're going nowhere fast. Unless I can engage the others, nothing is going to change. And I've tried to talk to them, but they're stonewalling me.

Coach: Just like you waited in the past until the president ran out of enthusiasm.

Kramer: Except this time there's more at stake. How do I get this train out of the station?

Coach: What's the main approach you've taken with the others so far?

Kramer: I've made it very clear that the future of the company is on the line.

Coach: And perhaps their jobs?

Kramer: I haven't come out and said that, but they get the message.

Coach: Fear is not the best way to stimulate innovation.

Kramer: You're saying I should approach the others in a different way.

Coach: Yes. Kramer, what makes *you* think creatively?

Kramer: Hmmm. I'm at my best when I'm having fun and not worried.

Coach: Worried about what?

Kramer: When I'm not worried that my job is on the line. When I'm not worried yet about whether an idea will work. I'd rather figure that out later, and if it won't work I go on to some other idea.

I'm also more creative if I think my ideas will pay off for me. And when I've got other creative people helping me.

Coach: That all makes sense to me. People are usually at their most creative when they're enjoying it and not feeling threatened, and when they suspend judgment for a while. And most people are more creative when they're part of a creative team.

Kramer: So even though the company is losing market share and there's some real threat here, I'm probably turning off the team's creativity by emphasizing that threat.

Coach: Probably.

Kramer: So I need to find a way to get the team to see that they'll benefit from this innovation, and I've got to find a way to make it exciting.

Coach: You're much more likely to stimulate the innovation the president is looking for.

Kramer: I get it.

Coach: And one more thing. Even if the president has made his mark on that previously blank piece of paper, there's still a lot of blank space left.

Kramer: I get the message. I'll check it out and see what happens. Gotta go see my herbalist. See you next month.

(*One month later . . .*)

Coach: Welcome back. Would you close the door, please?

Kramer: Sure, no problem. Listen, you wouldn't believe what's happened since we last talked. I pulled my team together and used an entirely different strategy. Or maybe it was the herbs.

Coach: What happened?

Kramer: I really prepared for the first meeting. I wrote down all the conditions that stimulate me to innovate. Just like we talked. Fun, security, freedom to brainstorm, what's-in-it-for-me, teamwork, and I added one more.

Coach: What did I overlook?

Kramer: Food.

Coach: Of course.

Kramer: I brought in bagels, fruit, punch, cheese — and it worked! We all relaxed and had a few laughs before I said anything about the new project. Then I told everyone that even though the industry is getting more competitive, we're not in hot water yet. We're still very profitable.

But I also said we have a challenge in front of us to create new products for stressed-out parents. I said I thought we could come up with something really new. And I reminded them of some of the additional stock options and other bonuses we've received in the past when something new really succeeded. I had them all fired up at first.

Coach: Wow! Then what happened?

Kramer: Well, I told them about the president's idea. The Mobile Electronic Sensor System. You know, the M.E.S.S.

Coach: How did they respond?

Kramer: They started whining and complaining about the whole concept. They said it would never sell. They said it was too complicated to coordinate orders from a web site with customized recording of parents' voices.

Finally, I stepped in and told them that all of their objections were valid, but that this was only a starting point. I said the president gave us a mostly blank piece of paper to work on, and that I believed in our teams and was convinced we would all benefit big time if we could come up with something truly innovative.

Coach: How did they respond?

Kramer: They just sat there for a minute. Nobody said anything.

Coach: And what did you do at that moment?

Kramer: That's when I had the ice cream delivered. Everybody laughed, and Elaine said she knew I was up to something. But I said, "No, *we* are up to something! Let's have some fun and let the ideas flow. We'll save the reality testing for later."

Coach: You got them brainstorming. Great! What happened next?

Kramer: Silence at first. But finally someone said, "Okay, I've got a couple of ideas. Although I think the idea of a mobile sensing system is just crazy, maybe we could come up with something else that appeals to our traditional customer base — kids — as well as their stressed-out parents. Like some sort of video game in which the kid earns points by hitting the moving potty. We can take advantage of our existing know-how in game software and break into the frustrated parent market, just like the president wants. And it's easy to customize software."

Coach: How did you respond?

Kramer: I said, "Good idea," and jumped up to the flip chart to write it down. Then I turned to the rest of the group and asked, "Can we add to this idea or build on it in some way?"

Then someone else jumped in and said, "Well, the idea of a video game makes me think of other CD applications. How about a Teletubbie-Goes-Potty CD-ROM? Use natural role models to teach the kids and attract the parents. It could be customized by superimposing an image of the child into the face of one of the Teletubbies."

So I wrote that down and said, "Keep going. We're on a roll."

Then someone else chimed in and said, "If we're going to start producing video CDs, let's do digital audio, too. How about a nighttime tape library for little kids? Use sleep-teaching methods to imprint potty-training messages on their little brains. We could semi-customize it by offering the messages in several different cartoon character voices."

That sparked someone else to say we were getting too far away from the original idea of actual potty-training methods. She got totally excited and said, "How about high-tech reusable diapers? They would alert the child to minor setbacks by providing a physically harmless jolt of electric current. In order to remind the sensitive parent — our actual customer — of the higher purpose behind the child's temporary distress, we could customize each one with the parent's favorite supportive clichés printed on the panties, like 'no pain, no gain' or 'this hurts me more than it hurts you,' or whatever."

Coach: Great! Okay, I get the picture. Let's move on.

Kramer: No, wait. There's more. The next person stood up and screamed, "IN-FO-MER-CIALS! I can see it now! We could have a series of them: one for the M.E.S.S. contraption, one for the digital CD sleep-teaching library, one for the video games, one for the diapers, etc.

"For the M.E.S.S. contraption we could hire professors from M.I.T. to explain it. For the digital CD sleep-teaching library we could feature Buzz Lightyear encouraging parents to trust technology and give it a try. For the video games we could have Bill Gates talk about how busy he is and how much this new software helped his kids' potty-training progress. For the reusable electrified diapers we could get parents to talk about how good they feel about not filling up landfills with disposable diapers."

And the guy was almost screaming when he said, "These infomercials build on the president's idea to begin with. You know he'll go for it!"

Coach: How did the group respond to all of this?

Kramer: They went wild! Everybody started talking at once. We were taping flip charts full of ideas all over the wall. It went on for two hours!

Then about halfway through, the manufacturing folks started chiming in. I was sure they'd be killjoys, but they talked about how we could set up manufacturing using focused factories for each product line, with work cells and work teams for each product.

And if we could limit customized options to a certain number of voices or printed messages, we could use a just-in-time process to respond to daily orders from the web site. Customer orders could be sent out with a two-day turnaround time, just like the president suggested.

Coach: Where did this discussion end up?

Kramer: Since that first meeting we've had several more. We've moved beyond brainstorming and realize that all these ideas need to be tested and researched for practicality and profitability.

So we've broken up into sub-teams. One group is looking into product possibilities. One group is researching the infomercial options. And the third group is working on manufacturing and distribution.

We'll meet every day for about two hours until we get a proposal together. Then we'll present it to the president when he gets back from the west coast.

Coach: You'll certainly have something good to say the next time the president asks, which is what you felt so much pressure about a month ago.

Kramer: You're right about that. I've gone from feeling stressed-out to not being able to wait to get back to work every morning. I'm firing on all cylinders. Yabba-dabba-do!

Coach: What made the difference for you?

Kramer: For one thing, I told everybody to produce or get off the potty, so to speak. Before that, I had all of the responsibility on my shoulders. Too much pressure.

Second, I challenged them to think for themselves in-stead of just shooting holes in someone else's ideas. And that it was okay for the creative process to be fun.

Third, I actually listened to them and let them throw out whatever ideas they had, good or bad. Once they real-ized I was taking their opinions seriously, they just kept going and started feeding off each other. It was amazing.

Coach: What did you learn from this experience?

Kramer: That there's a lot more to stimulating innovation than just telling people to come up with some new ideas.

Coach: Well, I think our time is about up.

Kramer: Yeah. Catch you later.

☑ PERSONAL DEVELOPMENT SUGGESTIONS

Delete "killer phrases" from your vocabulary. They block innovative thinking. Killing off an idea is as easy as not watering a seed. Avoid knee-jerk comments like:
- "It's a good idea, but..."
- "That's not our problem."
- "The old way works just fine."

Challenge your own thinking and ways of doing things.
Your team needs to see you as receptive to change and innovation. You can show it by challenging your own ideas. Ask yourself and your team questions that challenge the current way of doing things, such as:
- "Why do we do it this way?"
- "What could we change that would enhance what we're currently doing?"
- "If we could wave a wand and change one thing, what would it be? Why?"

Make short brainstorming sessions a regular habit.
Identify subjects that you and your team can take 5-10 minutes to brainstorm a list of ideas, questions, problems, solutions or alternatives about the subject at hand. The basic rules are:
1. Anyone can offer an idea.
2. No criticism.
3. Record them for all to see. It's easy to do and a great way to pool ideas.

Take on a difficult and challenging project. Find an assignment that stretches you and your team to find new solutions. Create an environment that fosters original thinking and collaboration. Do not let the risk of failure discourage you too much. Your team will grow from the experience, regardless of the outcome.

To gain insight, ask yourself these questions:

- Does your team have a stated vision? Can you explain it? Do you believe in it?

- How do you foster new ideas and innovative thinking in your team? How do you and your team react when confronted with problems and obstacles?

Practice a mindset that will help you stimulate innovation:

- *"It's my job to create excitement for what we are doing."*

- *"Every obstacle is a challenge to be overcome."*

- *"People will implement changes better if they help create them."*

Chapter 4

TRUSTING THE TEAM

"Thank you, Holliwell. I knew I could
count on you to correct my pronunciation."

What is trusting the team?

Trusting the team is the foundation of team-building. It is the groundwork for creating and coordinating a sustainable group of people. Such a group is able to play off each other's strengths while working together toward common goals.

As we have mentioned before, the word "team" refers to any group that works together to achieve goals, including project teams, research teams, self-directed work teams, cross-functional teams, virtual teams, global business teams, e-commerce teams, management teams, crews, staffs, boards, committees, etc. The list could go on.

Trusting the team requires a team leader who can think beyond the individual. It requires a leader who can think in terms of synergy, who can appreciate that the whole is greater than the sum of its parts.

Why is trusting the team so important?

None of this means that individual talents or specialties are ignored. To the contrary, the team leader notices who excels at a particular activity and channels that ability toward the greater good of the team and its goals. The leader trusts that an individual's strengths are more valuable in the context of a team than in isolation.

Today, most goals and projects are so complex that single individuals simply cannot meet and handle them. Success requires a group of people who can collaborate.

In the future, organizations will rely more and more on teams as their basic building blocks. The type, function and scope of teams will constantly transform to meet the ever-changing demands of the marketplace. Consequently, people will find themselves on a variety of teams during the course of their careers.

To develop and sustain highly effective teams, leaders must involve members in sharing information, solving problems and making decisions. All of that takes trust.

> "Over time, your team will trust you exactly as much as you trust your team."

◈ PROFILE OF A SUCCESSFUL TEAM LEADER

Ten tips for developing trust within your team:

1. **Demonstrate trust by encouraging team members to work together.** When members of a team see that you trust cooperation, the members themselves are more likely to trust working together.

2. **Put team goals above individual goals.** All members of the team must put accomplishing team goals ahead of their personal agendas. This makes for hard choices. If you do not set the example here, there is little hope the team will do so. In the end, everyone's success is tied to the success of the team.

3. **Abide by team norms and guidelines.** Most teams will agree on certain rules and norms that define group member's expectations of each other. The function of such norms is to assist in creating a trusting environment that helps the group stay focused. Conscientious leaders make sure appropriate norms are established and followed.

4. **Interact well with different personalities.** Teams are typically made up of very different people. This makes it challenging to understand, communicate and work together. If you can learn to appreciate and trust team members who are different from you, you can build high-performing teams based on each member's strengths.

5. **Help the team address and resolve problems.** When opportunities arise for cooperation or team problem solving, leaders must be ready to step in and facilitate. When issues are raised, make sure people listen to each other, share ideas and reach consensus whenever possible. Team members will trust you to assist and empower them to solve problems rather than dictate solutions.

6. **Ask for team input before making hiring or assignment decisions.** Deciding who will be a member of the team and what each member will do are two of the decisions that have the most direct impact on the whole team. Smart leaders solicit input from everyone before these decisions get made. This builds trust.

7. **Support decisions made by the team.** If the team has been given the authority to make certain decisions, it is imperative that the team leader supports such decisions once they are made. To override or veto team decisions sends the signal that the leader does not trust the team's judgment. The costs of a loss of trust are resentment and cynicism among team members.

8. **Recognize excellence and effort, and express praise.** When a goal is achieved or a project succeeds, good leaders seek out ways to reinforce the whole team's efforts. One of the surest ways to destroy trust is to make people feel taken for granted. As a leader, acknowledge the contribution of each

team member and how it assisted in the success. This highlights the team concept and the benefits of cooperation. It also increases pride, motivation and trust.

9. **Represent the team effectively to the rest of the organization.** No team works in a vacuum from the rest of the organization. You will be more effective if you make sure the rest of the organization has current information about team projects. If team members believe they are being misrepresented or undervalued by the larger organization, trust and morale will suffer.

10. **Treat team members with courtesy and respect.** Most people invest a lot of themselves in their work. They need the respect of their leaders. When leaders treat team members with courtesy and respect, they usually respond with loyalty and increased trust.

> "One of the surest ways to destroy trust is to make people feel taken for granted."

⊙ DIALOGUE WITH AN EXECUTIVE COACH

"Everything that's worthwhile comes with some risk."

Sam is the operations manager for a company that manufactures a wide range of telecommunication devices. The company has a management team of seven team leaders and several additional staff members. The business is experiencing extremely rapid growth with severe demands on operations to meet aggressive delivery dates.

Coach: Good morning, Sam. It's been a while since we talked.

Sam: Yes, several weeks. Hello, Rob. It's been insane around here. Would you like a cup of coffee?

Coach: Sure. Thanks.

Sam: E-commerce will either make us all rich or put us in an early grave. My department is getting stressed to the breaking point. Have a seat. New orders are coming much faster than we ever anticipated, and the sales department is promising our customers unrealistic delivery dates. We're working around the clock, seven days a week to meet the demand. We can't afford to get behind.

Coach: Success is stressful.

Sam: Yeah, but it beats failure.

Coach: I imagine people's nerves are a bit frayed.

Sam: Stress is one thing. This is a competitive business, and we're all used to that. And in our first 360 feedback session, you told me my people like me for my motivation and drive. So I don't think this is about stress. I think there's something else going on, and that's what I want to focus on today.

Coach: Good! So tell me what's happening.

Sam: It's hard to describe, Rob, but I'm noticing much more resistance from my team leaders on several issues. Normally they jump on an idea and fly with it — I've got a great bunch of people here. But lately, they sort of ignore me, or they halfheartedly debate an issue, particularly if it's me who brings it up. I just don't get it. It's like I've lost some of the respect I worked so hard to build up over the past three years.

Coach: Assuming you're right, any theories on why you've lost some respect?

Sam: That's what I can't figure out. I work longer hours than anybody in the department. If somebody's got a problem, I'm there to help. If I make a mistake, I don't cover it up. That's how I built respect with the others and that's still the way I operate.

Coach: It's true that nothing in the 360 indicated that people are questioning your commitment or your support for others.

Sam: Exactly. There have been a few times I've lost my temper — I admit it — and I wondered if that's been making people feel different about me. But I don't think that's it, either.

Coach: Nobody seemed to have an issue with that in your 360.

Sam: Right. I think it's because when it happens, I apologize. I talk through the situation. There are managers here who blow up and then act like it doesn't matter. So if anything, I think the fact that I get angry and then acknowledge it and talk it out probably increases people's respect for me.

Coach: That's very plausible. So far it doesn't sound like you think you need to improve or change your demonstration of commitment or how you handle strong emotions on the job.

Sam: That's how I see it. But you're the coach. You've studied the 360 feedback report, and you've talked to some of my colleagues. What do you think?

Coach: I'm with you. I have not heard a pattern of feedback that would make me think these are the areas to worry about.

Sam: Good. Because I'm driving everybody pretty hard right now, but my assumption is that everybody knows what's at stake.

Coach: What do you mean by "what's at stake"?

Sam: The company's stock is doing fabulous. Sales and income have doubled for two years in a row. And if we can keep this up for another year, there's a good chance the company will be a takeover candidate and our future will be . . . well, the potential is enormous. We all win big.

Coach: And what's at stake for you, Sam? Besides the fortune.

Sam: There's a good chance I'll be made vice president. Wait a minute. Do you think they might be jealous?

Coach: They're human beings. Is there a reason for them to be jealous?

Sam: For about the last month, I've been leaving early a couple times a week to handle some personal business. I've heard a couple of joking remarks by one of my team members implying I'm out politicking for the VP job. I blew off the comments. Or maybe I just didn't want to consider the implications.

Coach: Say more . . .

Sam: Do I have to spell it out, Rob? It's hard enough to be black and in management without some rumor going around about wanting special treatment or about playing politics. My team ought to know me better than that. That's just not the way I am.

Coach: Have you told them what you are doing when you leave early?

Sam: No.

Coach: Why not?

Sam: It's complicated.

Coach: Okay . . .

Sam: Well, my daughter has some kind of strange virus — it could be very serious — and she has to go to the hospital for treatments twice a week for a couple of hours. This is very hard for her.

Coach: And for you?

Sam: Yes, but she's only ten and she's very afraid. I'm the only one she'll go with.

Coach: I'm sure most people would be sympathetic.

Sam: Maybe. But I still think too many people could misinterpret the situation.

Coach: Perhaps. But if they don't know the facts, they'll speculate. And that's almost sure to lead to misunderstanding. It seems like making a choice to tell them about your situation — even if there's some risk there — is more likely to *avoid* misunderstanding.

Sam: There's another level of this I don't think you can really understand.

Coach: Let me try.

Sam: It's this. Like I said, being black on this job is hard enough. But being a woman in a leadership position makes it even tougher. I feel as if I'm already swimming upstream. I don't want to raise the working mom issue on top of everything else. Not now, anyway. Not when I've got a real chance to be a vice president and break the glass ceiling.

Coach: Samantha, let me see if I do understand. You've worked very hard to get where you are. You feel that your race and gender have been disadvantages for you to overcome. And you think being a working mother with child care concerns is another major disadvantage. And that you're probably out of the running for VP."

Sam: Okay, you've got that part, Rob. At least intellectually. But I can't imagine you know what that really feels like on a daily basis —

Coach: I'm sure you're right about that.

Sam: I don't think you can begin to understand what's at stake for me. I'm the first person in my family to graduate from college — with an engineering degree of all things. I also helped my younger brothers and sisters get through school.

Sam: You're saying this is about more than your career or your income or even your job.

Sam: Yes. Much more. To be an officer in a company like this at my age is a rare thing. I could show my family and my people that a good education and hard work can pay off, no matter where you start. I just can't afford to take too many chances right now.

Coach: You have quite a dilemma, Sam. On one side, you're trying not to risk your career. And even more than that, you're trying not to risk a statement you want to make with your life. On the other side, you're risking the trust of your team.

Sam: The trust of the team?

Coach: I think so. Whether or not this is about the team's *respect*, it is certainly about their *trust*.

Sam: How so?

Coach: You don't trust them enough to tell them why you're leaving early. They're left to guess, and judging from your comments about people ignoring you and suddenly debating your ideas more than they used to, I'd say your hunch is right that they think this is about politics rather than being a devoted parent. While there is no *real* reason for them not to trust you, their *perception* that you're keeping something from them is enough to stir up rumors and damage trust.

Sam: I can see that.

Coach: So my question as your coach is this: what do you want to change or improve?

Sam: I would just like things to be easy for once.

Coach: I agree this is unfair. You face high risk in both directions. But I'm going to push you here. What do you want from your team?

Sam: I want them to trust me.

Coach: Why is that important to you?

Sam: I want them to trust me because that's the way I do business. I'm not a politician. I don't ask for special treatment. I earn what I get. And I want my team and this company to be incredibly successful.

Coach: The trust of your team is a basic value of yours.

Sam: Absolutely, but I'm trying to play both sides of the fence because I'm worried that if I tell my team enough to reestablish trust, I might do so at the expense of upper management's assessment of my suitability for the VP position.

Coach: So what you're doing at this point in order to play both sides of the fence, as you put it, is to keep the situation with your daughter to yourself and keep your fingers crossed that your team won't misjudge you.

Sam: I hate it when you lay things out so clearly. But yes. That's what I'm doing now.

Coach: And is what you're doing now working?

Sam: No. It's not.

Coach: So what could you do differently?

Sam: As we talk through it, I can see I really need to tell my team leaders about my trips to the hospital. It makes me angry that some of the folks upstairs may view that as a negative when it comes to making me a VP, but I guess I'm going to have to cross that bridge later.

Coach: When will you tell your team?

Sam: We have a meeting tomorrow morning at ten. I might as well do it then. The sooner the better from my point of view.

Coach: What do you think will happen?

Sam: It's definitely a risk. But everything that's worthwhile in this life comes with some risk. The bottom line for me is if I can't be honest with my fellow workers, they won't trust me and I won't respect myself. I guess that's what counts.

Coach: What support do you need?

Sam: I don't know. You've supported me by helping to clarify some things. This is what I said I wanted to focus on, and we did. And now I'm clear about what I need to do.

Coach: Clarity is good.

Sam: Yes, clarity is good. But this is still hard.

Coach: Call me if you feel like letting me know how the team meeting went.

Sam: Thanks.

☑ PERSONAL DEVELOPMENT SUGGESTIONS

Observe yourself in action; analyze your own behavior. The next time you are working for important team results, notice what you do to encourage people to work together. Do you express the need for teamwork in a way that motivates people to action? Do you look for ways to increase trust?

Explain your expectations of the team in concrete terms. Explain to the team exactly what kind of team effort is required for success, along with your expectations. For example: "Folks, we simply must keep each other better informed when customers call to make changes." Don't let your expectations be vague or go unspoken. Communication builds trust.

Praise and reinforce team effort and results whenever warranted. Give credit and recognition only when it is earned. When you give praise, be very specific about what aspects of someone's work mattered most. For example: "I just want to thank everyone who stayed late last night to get the project completed on time. Your willingness to jump in and help made the difference."

Ask your team what the barriers are to better teamwork. Have a brainstorming session to answer the question, "What is standing in our way to being a high-performing team?" List them all on the board and have the team rank them from most important to least important. Ask them to identify what you might be doing that is a barrier to better teamwork. Say something like, "If there is something I am doing or not doing which you think is getting the way, feel free to let me know."

Adapt your style to encourage different people to talk with you. If you wish to "connect" with people who are not like you, adapt your communication style in a way that is most comfortable to them. Simple questions like "How's it going?" will usually set the stage. At the end of conversations, a statement like "It's been good talking with you" or "Thanks for telling me" will reinforce the idea that you want people to communicate with you.

To gain insight, ask yourself these questions:

- Think of a time when you belonged to a group where teamwork was not practiced or actively encouraged. How did you feel? What impact did this have on the level of cooperation among the members of the group?

- What are the norms of your team? Which norm would your team members like you to pay more attention to? Do any of your words or actions violate the letter or the spirit of team guidelines?

Practice a mindset that will help you trust the team:

- *"Trust is a two-way street."*

- *"None of us is as smart as all of us."*

- *"I will be successful if I trust capable people to do a good job."*

Chapter 5

EMPOWERED DECISION-MAKING

"I feel I should warn you, sir. Budlong, in personnel,
is starting a pro-democracy movement."

What does it mean to empower team decisions?

Empowered decision-making is the process of getting people highly involved in making decisions that affect them. It means letting them actually make the decision when appropriate, or at least soliciting their input when the decision must be made at a higher level.

Not every decision can be made by a consensus of the team members. At times, the leader must step in and decide. In other cases, decisions may be delegated to a single person or small group of people who study a problem and render a decision.

The team leader has a twofold challenge:
- to help determine which type of decision-making is most appropriate in any given situation (consensus of the entire team, majority vote, decision by committee, etc.)
- to put the appropriate people together with the right information so an effective decision can be made and implemented

Why is it important to empower team decisions?

Empowered decision-making is based on the principle that when people participate in a decision, they are more invested in its outcome.

There is no such thing as a perfect decision. When decisions are implemented, there are always obstacles to overcome along the way. Nonetheless, when you empower the team to make decisions, you increase the likelihood that team members will fully commit to the decision (less discouragement, less resistance, less sabotage). When people feel like they have "ownership" of a decision, they also feel more accountable — and they work harder to overcome barriers to success.

Literally, empowering someone means giving him or her power. Power has traditionally been thought of as a limited resource to be guarded by those who have it. If you can think of power as the ability to orchestrate people and resources in order to get things done, then power becomes an expanding resource. Sharing it, not hoarding it, enhances everyone's power.

> "When people participate in a decision, they are more invested in its outcome."

◈ PROFILE OF A SUCCESSFUL TEAM LEADER

Ten tips for successfully empowering team decision-making:

1. **Define the goals and explain why they are important.** People invest more of themselves when they are clear about what they are trying to achieve and why it is important. Knowing "why" gives people a better understanding of the desired outcomes. It encourages them to think of creative ways to achieve the objective.

2. **Solicit input from team members on decisions.** By consulting with the team, leaders help members feel ownership in the decision. People are more likely to give input freely if they believe it is desired and valued. Smart leaders inspire team members to contribute ideas and opinions by asking for them, listening to them, using them and giving credit where credit is due.

3. **"Let go" and let the team decide, when appropriate.** Although not every decision can be made by the team, wise team leaders will let the team decide whenever possible. You will get far better results from your team if you look for ways to increase everyone's feelings of ownership and accountability in decision-making.

4. **Delegate projects and decisions based on the strengths of individual team members.** Everyone

does not have the same set of skills and strengths. To get maximum contribution from all team members, good leaders will assign responsibility based on the strengths of individual members.

5. **Avoid making decisions for the team or for a member to whom responsibility has been assigned.** When you grant responsibility and authority, you must be prepared to trust people to make good decisions and carry out relevant tasks. People will lose confidence and trust if you hover over them, require approval for every decision or step in to do things for them.

6. **Explain how much authority has been given and clearly define the boundaries.** It is important to clarify how much freedom has been authorized, and to provide guidelines for a given decision (such as nonnegotiable items or specific constraints). This lets the team know how much "rope" it has and where the "fences" are located.

7. **Weigh the pros and cons of several options before deciding.** There are no perfect solutions. Effective team leaders look for several options, then weigh the pros and cons of each option. This motivates everyone to consider issues from several perspectives and to draw on diverse insights, which results in more effective and creative solutions.

8. **Take appropriate risks when necessary.** You can never exactly predict the consequences of a decision.

But the more significant the potential consequences, the greater the risk. By anticipating potential consequences of a decision, you can make better judgments concerning risk levels, and you can decide whether the risk is worth taking to achieve your overall objectives.

9. **Go outside the team for ideas and resources when needed.** Smart team leaders learn about important links to the rest of the organization and develop positive relationships with people in other areas. When necessary, the leader can reach out for information, suggestions, and other resources to support the team in its decision-making efforts.

10. **Evaluate the practicality of decisions.** A decision is worthless if it can't be implemented. Effective team leaders pay attention not only to the apparent quality of the decision but also to the probability that it can be implemented successfully.

> "Power is an expanding resource.
> The more you share it, the
> greater your ability to get things
> done."

⊙ DIALOGUE WITH AN EXECUTIVE COACH

"How do you decide how to decide?"

David is a team leader for an Atlanta-based medical imaging technology firm. His team has stayed intact through two mergers and was even relocated together during the second merger. This coaching session takes place by telephone.

Coach: Good morning, David.

David: 'Morning, George.

Coach: How's the weather today in the Peach Tree State?

David: It's supposedly sunny and mild, but here in Munich it's raining.

Coach: You're in Germany?

David: Corporate gave us two hours yesterday to get a team rep on a plane. They're trying to develop a strategic alliance with a company over here and suddenly decided they wanted an engineer to meet with one of the German teams to see if we could collaborate on an important product.

Coach: What's up?

David: I had time on the plane to think more about the results of my 360 feedback report. I'd like to focus on the part about decision-making.

Coach: Okay. I've got the file open. I'm reading some of your team's comments about your decision-making style.

David: Yeah. I've got that on my screen, too. More than one team member has made a comment to the effect that I'm decisive to a fault.

Coach: Other members of the organization outside your team made similar comments.

David: Well, I expect that sort of remark from the HR team and some of the support staff. Hell, I'm an engineer. I'm Dilbert to them. I've heard all my life that I'm a computer thinly disguised as a human being. But when my team members say it — other engineers — I don't know what to make of it. But I do take it seriously, and I want to understand it so I can make some changes.

Coach: What do you want to change?

David: I can't say exactly, but it's something about how we as a team make decisions. I want that to improve.

Coach: Why? What makes that important?

David: I know the world is changing rapidly. The way I make decisions worked fine in the Navy and in other jobs. But if it's time to update, it's time.

Coach: David, we've been talking on and off for three months now. I have to say this: I don't buy what you're saying. I think there's more.

David: Yeah. You're right. Look, no offense, coach, but there's another part of me that thinks this is all nonsense. Sometimes I think if all the coaches and the consultants and the HR types would just leave my team and me alone, we'd come out of the lab once in a while with something amazing. Somebody else can make big money off of our innovations, pay us something decent and let us disappear back into the lab.

Coach: That's exactly why I want to know why this is important to *you*. What purpose of *yours* will be served by this intended change in decision-making? You won't really make any substantial and lasting changes if you're doing it to save your job or to get somebody off your back. So what's your ultimate objective for improving the team's decision-making? What's your purpose?

David: I'm proud of my team. We have contributed to the creation of some extraordinary technology. We've definitely advanced the technical side of medicine. And we've outlasted the company that brought us together. I want to see us go even further.

Coach: You want to improve your team's decision-making ability because you can see even greater inventions in the future.

David: That's really what I want. Better decisions will make for better engineering.

Coach: Good. That's why we're talking. That's what this is all about. So let's talk about how you and your team currently make decisions. Let's start there.

David: Fine. As engineers, we analyze a situation or a problem. We break it down into parts. We generate logical alternatives. We run scenarios. We weigh probabilities. We go with the option most likely to accomplish the end goal.

Coach: Okay. That sounds pretty functional. Let me ask you this. When we started this call, did I hear you say that corporate gave the team two hours to get somebody on a plane to Munich?

David: That's right.

Coach: Is that exactly what happened? It sounds like the team had a decision to make quickly, and that the decision had pretty wide parameters. Any member of the team could be in Germany right now. Not necessarily the leader. Right?

David: Well, I guess so . . .

Coach: So the team analyzed the situation, generated a list of people who could make the trip, weighed the pros and cons of each alternative, and then as an entity chose you? Is that how it happened?

David: Wait a minute. I was referring to the big decisions. Technical stuff. This trip is stressful, but I'll be home tomorrow night. The team is at a crucial phase in a project, and my role at this point is less "hands on" than the other members. It just made sense for me to go.

Coach: That may well be. But I'm focusing on the decision-making *process*. What was the team's process in sending you overseas as opposed to some other member of the team?

David: I took the call from upstairs. I wanted to use time efficiently so as not to interrupt the team's work. The decision seemed obvious. I made it.

Coach: As you look at the rest of this 360 feedback report, David, what "fault" do you think your colleagues are referring to when they say that you are "decisive to a fault"?

David: Okay, I see where we're heading.

Coach: Where are we heading?

David: Involving others in my decisions.

Coach: *Whose* decisions?

David: Well, yes. Of course. They're *our* decisions. But look, we could sit around wasting time all day if we talked every decision to death. We make hundreds of decisions every week.

Coach: And how do you decide how to decide?

David: I'm getting a little lost. Help me out here.

Coach: Have you and your team ever sat down and simply talked about what method you want to use in making decisions? Big ones. Little ones. Decisions on short notice, like who jumps on a plane. Long-term decisions, like who is going to focus on a specific aspect of a project.

David: Well, no. That seems . . . unnecessary.

Coach: How so?

David: It's like talking about how to breathe. Decision-making and problem solving is what we do all the time. That's how our minds work. And besides, I suspect my team members would probably say they don't care about most of the little decisions.

Coach: Was the trip to Germany a little decision or a big decision?

David: I thought of it as a little one.

Coach: That may be true. But this 360 seems to be saying that many people feel your decisiveness, while on the one hand a strength, sometimes leaves them feeling undervalued or ignored.

David: If that's true, it's certainly not my intention. It's just that a lot of people depend on me to be decisive. At work and at home. I don't mean to be callous, but I can't be worrying about all the feelings of the people I work with. Not on top of everything else I'm trying to accomplish.

Coach: That makes sense. Let me summarize: You want to improve how your team makes decisions because you believe it will lead to even greater inventions. But you're not exactly sure what those changes need to be.

You have a method by which you've made thousands of decisions in your life, and your team members make hundreds every week, and most of those decisions turn out quite well. You're getting messages from various sources that people want to be more involved in decisions, but it's not yet clear how they want to be involved, or how much. Am I in the ballpark?

David: So far so good.

Coach: Then I propose an experiment. When you get back, call a team meeting. Plan it far enough ahead that you can do a breakfast or a lunch. Give yourselves some time. Make sure the food is good.

David: Why is that important?

Coach: The experimental conditions have to be just right if you want to get quality data.

David: Right. I know just the place.

Coach: Or you could start the experiment with the restaurant choice. Ask the team for suggestions. See if they're interested in a minor decision like where to eat.

David: I got it.

Coach: Then, when you're all relaxed, and you've told them how good the bratwurst was in Munich and how no place in Atlanta can come close to it, you move into a discussion about the future of the team. Tell them what you've told me — that the team is pretty amazing but you want to take things even further. And as part of this discussion about the future, ask them if they want to make any changes in how decisions are made.

David: Just come out and ask them?

Coach: Yeah, but it's *how* you ask them. You have to do it *your* way, David. Whatever that is.

David: I'd probably say something like, "I've read what all of you said about me in the 360 feedback report. Anybody want to step outside?"

Coach: I'm sure that will get you want you need.

David: But seriously, how about, uh, "I'm interested in improving our decision-making. I think we're great individual decision-makers, but we've never discussed how we do it as a team. Let's look at this the way we look at a machine. How does it work? How could it work better?" Something like that, maybe?

Coach: Perfect.

David: Then what do I do?

Coach: Then you stay quiet for as long as you can stand it. They might not say much for a little while. Things might seem awkward at first. But the very fact that you're asking the question will empower the team. Even if you don't get a whole lot of information during that first discussion, you've initiated an experiment.

Over a few weeks you'll get some important new knowledge. Including some feedback on what size of a decision team members want to be involved in. You'll find out when they want you to make the decision, and when they want to be involved.

Then come back and we'll crunch the data, so to speak, and together we can refine our focus as to what changes you may or may not want to make.

David: This sounds logical and practical.

Coach: Coming from you, that's high praise. I'll see you when you get back to the states.

☑ PERSONAL DEVELOPMENT SUGGESTIONS

Catalogue the types of decisions made in your area.
Make a list of the various types of decisions your team
makes (such as hiring new members, job assignments,
quality approvals, new equipment purchases, etc.) List
who is currently responsible for each type of decision, as
well as who provides input. Look for ways to expand decision-making authority to more team members.

**Discuss and formalize the decision-making process in
your team.** Talk to your team members about how decisions are now made. Show them your list of types of decisions and who makes them. Ask them what decisions
they feel they could make in the future. Figure out what
information or training they would need to transfer decision-making responsibility to the team.

Improve the fit between people and assignments.
When assigning projects or tasks to individuals, try and
build on the strengths of individual members. Consider
these criteria when making assignments:
- Does the person's capabilities fit the need?
- Does the person want the assignment?
- Did the customer request this person?
- Will the assignment help this person learn and
  develop?

Cross-train team members. Help the team members
learn about each other's responsibilities and problems.
They will gain a greater appreciation for everyone's role.
When it comes time to make decisions, each member will

bring a broader perspective to the decision, leading to better dialogues and decisions.

To gain insight, ask yourself these questions:

- Do you have a low, medium or high need for control? How do you show it?

- Do you willingly transfer decision-making authority to others? Or do you find reasons for holding on and reserving that power for yourself? Why?

Practice a mindset that will help you empower team decisions:

- *"People are not part of the organization. They are the organization."*

- *"All of us are smarter than any one of us."*

- *"When I give people the power to fail, I empower them to learn."*

Chapter 6

NURTURING DIALOGUE

"Say what's on your mind, Harris—the language of dance has always eluded me."

What does it mean to nurture dialogue?

Dialogue is a specific form of conversation between two or more people. It is more than just an exchange of views. Its purpose is to openly examine beliefs and values so better solutions and fresh ways of thinking can emerge. Dialogue is achieved when everyone involved comes to a new level of understanding about the issue at hand. It is a practical tool.

Dialogue cannot be forced. It has to be nurtured, in-vited, and encouraged. Nurturing dialogue is the art of bringing different people together in a productive and creative exchange. Great team leaders help interactions between team members proceed more smoothly. By nur-turing dialogue, team leaders help people communicate in a way that leads to sound thinking and better decisions.

Why is nurturing dialogue so important?

Accurate information and sound reasoning are essential for a team to perform its job. If a team takes action based on assumptions or faulty reasoning, it is likely to waste resources and suffer setbacks.

While it is not essential that team members always agree, it *is* essential that they seek each other's best thinking. It is critical that team members share what they know and remain open to learning from one another.

Achieving this level of dialogue is difficult. Many people cling to their knowledge and opinions for a variety of reasons. Some people clutch their prejudices. Other people are naturally reserved and will not offer an opinion unless they are asked directly. Still others are afraid to speak up for fear of looking stupid. And some might view information as a source of power — not sharing it unless they believe they have some advantage to gain.

The best team leaders set the example for an open and free-flowing exchange of information and opinions. They help draw out each team member so the team gets full value from everyone.

> "Dialogue is the tool
> for connecting
> two minds."

◈ PROFILE OF A SUCCESSFUL TEAM LEADER

Ten tips for successfully nurturing dialogue:

1. **State your own opinions, paying attention to tact and timing.** It is important for all participants, including the leader, to share what they believe. As a leader, when you reveal what is on your mind you are likely to be perceived as honest and confident.

   Be conscious, however, of how and when you state your opinions. If you always speak first, you may discourage other team members from speaking. If you express yourself too forcefully, some members will think your mind is already made up. With tact and timing, there is a much better chance that people will consider your opinions in the spirit of dialogue.

2. **State your opinions *clearly*.** If you want people to truly understand you, clarity is a must. Simple, straightforward expression is usually best. Try to "get to the point" rather quickly, supporting your opinions with facts and concrete examples whenever possible.

3. **Explain the reasoning behind your opinions.** Smart leaders express their reasoning for the team to analyze and build upon. When you do this, your opinion is more likely to be understood or improved upon. You also encourage others to do the same.

4. **Ask others for feedback and evaluation of your own opinions.** Dialogue helps you examine and improve on your reasoning and assumptions. Encourage people to evaluate your opinions. Is your thinking as logical as it could be? Are your opinions based on good data? Are you overlooking something? By encouraging people to give you feedback, you create a climate where all ideas can be discussed and evaluated.

5. **Communicate without ridicule or threats.** You will inevitably hear things that are unpleasant or that you didn't expect to hear: disagreements, mistakes, team setbacks. Some information or feedback might be expressed in a clumsy or even hostile manner. It is important that you do not respond to bad news or criticism with any level of threats, sarcasm or ridicule.

   When faced with disagreement or bad news, the best leaders express openness to new thinking. Such a response helps people feel more comfortable challenging your reasoning or delivering unpleasant news.

6. **Ask others for their opinions.** Effective dialogue depends on *everyone* sharing opinions. Some people may be reluctant to share their thoughts if they think others will disagree — especially the leader. Take the initiative: solicit the opinions of others, and encourage them to volunteer their ideas in the future.

7. **Ask others for the reasoning behind their opinions.** Helping others explain their thinking gets them more involved in the dialogue and encourages them to evaluate their own conclusions. Take care not to discredit or dismiss opinions. Try to probe in a non-threatening way for the facts and assumptions behind opinions.

8. **Demonstrate a willingness to change your mind.** Nobody is perfect. Nobody has all the answers. Leaders who alter their opinions based on new information send a powerful message that good dialogue can change minds.

9. **Avoid point-counterpoint debates.** We hire attorneys because they are masters of debate. They are trained to win a legal contest. But most of the activity inside a team or organization is not a contest. Team objectives will not be reached if the leader simply debates the members.

   Debate can be a powerful and useful tool for some jobs. But it can be the wrong tool for the job when dealing with team conflicts, creativity, or personal relationship difficulties.

10. **Know when to be persuasive and when to be receptive.** It takes mental discipline to put your opinions on hold while carefully listening to someone else. If you are too quick to launch into a persuasive "pitch" for your opinion, you shut down the team's openness to dialogue. Persuasion is a powerful tool in

sales, in the courtroom, in politics. However, like debate, persuasion is sometimes the wrong tool for the job.

> "Dialogue is achieved when everyone comes to a new level of understanding."

⊙ DIALOGUE WITH AN EXECUTIVE COACH

"There's a difference between debate and dialogue."

Harold and Art work for a regional sporting goods firm based in Charlotte. Harold ran the marketing department until he was recently assigned to a ten-member team responsible for taking the company into e-commerce. Art joined the company three months ago after having successfully designed e-commerce web sites for several much smaller companies in the area.

Both men are both used to being in charge. This is their first experience of having to collaborate on a project. The CEO is quite upset that after three months the team is still disorganized and in conflict. An executive coach has been asked to help Harold and Art communicate more effectively. The following discussion takes place on a conference call between Art's office in Charlotte, Harold's condo in Myrtle Beach, and the coach's office in Raleigh.

Coach: Hello, Harold.

Harold: Good morning, Rob! Where's Art? Isn't Art supposed to be on this call?

Coach: Well, yes. We all agreed to a three-way discussion. I'm sure he'll call in any minute.

Harold: This is my vacation, after all. It's supposed to rain here this afternoon and I'd like to get out to the golf course as soon as I can.

Coach: I understand. And I appreciate your being willing to have this meeting while you're away.

Harold: No problem.

(*The phone rings; Art joins the conference call.*)

Art: Hi. Art here. Who's on the call?

Coach: We're both here, Art.

Art: Hi, Rob. Hello, Harold. Sorry I'm a little late.

Coach: You're both on a tight schedule today, so let's jump in. I've had a chance to talk to each of you separately, but your chief has asked me to meet with you together about what appears to him to be pretty significant communication problems on the e-commerce team.

Harold: That's a nice way to put it.

Coach: How would you put it, Harold?

Harold: Basically I don't think this team is going to work in the way it's currently set up. Art, don't take this personally, but I think the chief was too idealistic to make us do this as a team.

I'm all for the move to e-commerce, and I know you're an excellent web site designer and all that, but we've always done fine with a marketing department that leads the charge into new territories.

Art: And the dinosaurs did fine for about a thousand centuries until the whole world—

Harold: —Why do you instantly get sarcastic, Art?

Art: Probably for the same reason you get instantly condescending.

Harold: It just so happens that I've been with this company since—

Coach: Whoa! Hold on a minute! Harold, Art, as I was saying, your chief feels there are some pretty significant communication problems on the team. I vaguely remember him using the phrase "tension you can cut with a knife." Now I see what he means.

Harold: My point is that there is no way we are ever going to—

Coach: —Harold, time out. I need you to listen to me.

Art: Good luck, Rob. That's about as likely as—

Coach: Art, you too. I want both of you to be quiet or we'll just end the call.

Harold: Okay.

Art: Right.

Coach: You guys need help in two ways. You need a coach *and* a referee. So I'm going to play both roles for the next few minutes. It's clear that left on your own you'll just bicker. My job isn't to get you guys to like each other. My job is to help you communicate in a way that's helpful to the company and its mission. So I'll play referee by saying whose turn it is to speak, and I'll play coach by helping you communicate better with each other. Got the plan?

Art: Yeah.

Harold: Ten-four, coach.

Coach: Good. Harold, let's start again. How do you see the situation?

Harold: All right, it's like this. We have this successful company. Hugely successful, really. In thirty years we've gone from a tiny little mom and pop store to a company with 500 employees, ten outlets, two warehouses. I could go on and on. And we're still expanding into three other states.

Do we need to go the e-commerce route? I've told the chief we don't need to. A lot of companies are losing money through e-commerce. But I also know that if we do it right and we're patient, we could be even more successful with e-commerce. That's all fine.

But it's *how* we're doing it that I don't like. It's as if the chief is reorganizing the whole company. We had a winning formula, so why change it?

Coach: Okay, thanks. Art? How do you see it?

Art: Pretty different than Harold sees it. I disagree that the company had a winning formula. It's great that you were successful in Charlotte and that you're growing into Georgia and Florida and South Carolina.

But I see the e-commerce move as more than just a chance to further expand. I see it as a survival move, and I think the chief sees it that way too. We may be expanding, but our overall market share is gradually shrinking. Think ten years into the future and we're in big trouble. Heck, five years and we're in trouble.

Harold: Too simple. We had plans on the board for five more outlets across the south. The numbers have been great for the last two years.

Art: Not that great.

Harold: We offer quality. We've got customer loyalty.

Art: It's not deep loyalty. They'll jump ship as quickly as they can click a mouse.

Harold: You're very clever, Art. Very clever.

Art: And you're naïve, Harold.

Harold: Naïve? I've been in this business for —

Coach: Time out, guys! Time out, again! Lets name what you were just doing. Eventually you returned to bickering, but before you did, you started out in debate mode. Point-counterpoint. The object is to win, to score points, to persuade. Politicians and attorneys are the masters of this mode. It is a very valuable form of communication.

But it is limited. It can be the wrong tool for the job. And that's what is happening here.

Harold: What's the alternative?

Coach: Good question. And I'll answer it in a minute, but first let me ask both of you something. Has the team split into two camps?

Art: Yes, definitely.

Harold: I agree. We've got the computer folks and the designers looking to Art, and the marketing and idea people looking to me.

Art: And they are not getting along any better than Harold and me.

Coach: So there are really two teams.

Harold: And that's my point. I think this situation would work if we just admit we're trying to cram two departments into one.

Art: I think I'm starting to agree with Harold.

Harold: There's hope yet.

Coach: Okay then, consider this. The team is mirroring its leaders. As long as the two of you — the team leaders — are at war, so shall the team be.

Harold: Doesn't that prove my point? We need departments, not teams.

Coach: No, for three reasons. First of all, the chief is very committed to this. He believes strongly that an integrated team with shared leadership is going to be much more innovative and profitable in the long run. He believes such a team will be able to adapt more quickly to changing market conditions.

Second, there are a lot of companies whose success proves the chief's point. So now let's go back to your original question about an alternative.

Art: Wait a minute, Rob. You said there were three reasons Harold hadn't proved his point. What's the third?

Coach: Oh, the third reason — and I'll be blunt here — is that you haven't really tried to be a team. It sounds to me like both of you, and perhaps some of the other team members as well, have certain positions on things. You're stuck. Let me introduce you to another way of communicating that just might help.

Harold: I'll try anything at this point.

Art: Yeah. Let's go for it.

Coach: Okay. Harold, let's go back to you. But I want you to have a different goal in mind this time. As you describe how you see the situation, your goal will be to get Art to understand you. That means you have to tell him the *reasons* you see things the way you do and what is most *important* to you.

Harold: Okay, I'll try. It's like this, Art. I've been with the company since I was twenty-five. I was here almost at the beginning. And I didn't quit during a couple of lean years when a lot of other people jumped ship. And I stayed with it partly because I love sports and sporting goods, and partly because we've really built something here. Something I'm proud of.

Coach: Art, I want you to respond with only one goal: make Harold believe you understood what he said.

Art: I do understand. Really. I do. It's just that times are changing. What was successful thirty years ago — or even five years ago — won't necessarily work any more.

Coach: Harold, do you believe Art understands you?

Harold: Not a bit.

Coach: Art, what else can you say that will make Harold believe you really listened to his perspective without just getting ready to debate it.

Art: I think maybe Harold was telling me that he sees himself as having a lot more invested in this company than I do. I've been here three months; he's been here three decades. And he's telling me he loves the whole world of sports and sporting goods — it's not just another business to him. And he's proud of the company's success and the fact that he contributed to it.

Harold: Bingo!

Coach: Anything else you want Art to know? Anything about the current changes in the company?

Harold: Yeah. I'm trying to go along with them, but I have my doubts. I want to take this company further. But I'm concerned that time and money will be wasted by jumping on the e-commerce bandwagon.

Art: But it won't be wasted. The way things are —

Coach: Art, remember the goal.

Art: Oh, right. Harold, you're worried that . . . well, I guess you're worried your life's work will be compromised or even erased.

Harold: He got it that time.

Coach: Good. Now Art, I want you to give your perspective, with your only goal being to get Harold to understand you. And Harold, I want you to listen without preparing a counterargument.

Harold: I'll be a good boy.

Art: For me it's like this, Harold. I have to be honest with you. I couldn't care less about sporting goods per se. But I'm excited by the potential of the Internet. It's a whole new world for business, but it's also a new art form. And I love art that is functional.

I want to create the most dynamic and exciting and elegant web site possible. I want to get it right. I've created things for smaller companies, but this is a chance for me to go to a new level with my craft. And when we're arguing, or when you're rushing me, I'm either too nervous or too angry to do my best work.

Coach: Harold, you know your goal.

Harold: Right. Art cares about different things than I do. At least in terms of the product. He doesn't care about the best running shoe or the best tennis racket. His idea of a good time and good product is to create something beautiful. Art is an artist. Get it?

Coach: Art? Did *Harold* get it?

Art: Almost. He got the part about my wanting to create something elegant. But I'm not sure he understood another aspect that's very important to me.

Harold: You want it to work right. You're an artist *and* an engineer.

Art: Yes.

Coach: Good. That's one difference between debate and dialogue. In a dialogue both people are open. They're willing to risk being influenced by the other person. My sense is that both of you understand the other better than you did half an hour ago.

Harold: That's true.

Art: Yes.

Coach: Now I'd like to hear from both of you where you think you share common ground.

Harold: Well, I realize we both want to be proud of the outcome of our project.

Art: Yes. And we both are trying to build our careers, to stretch ourselves.

Harold: And we're both a little nervous about things.

Art: And in a way that I hadn't seen before, our success is tied to each other's success.

Coach: Good. So far, through interactive listening, you've gone beyond bickering and debate. Now I'd like each of you to ask for one thing from the other person.

Art: Harold, I'd like to ask you to not rush me so much. I'm not slow by any means, but I'll create my best work if you ask me how much time I need instead of pushing me to go faster. And I guess that extends to the chief. You've known him for thirty years. You can talk to him. He's a visionary, but he's an impatient visionary.

Harold: I can give you that. I can see what you're saying.

Coach: Harold, what do you want from Art? Just one thing for now.

Harold: I want Art to listen to my creative ideas. Maybe I'm a dinosaur, and maybe some of my ideas can't be translated into e-commerce, but then again maybe they can.

Art: Sure, I can do that. I can listen better.

Coach: Good. Now there's just one more thing. I believe the two of you can use dialogue again and again to work together better. And of course I'm available to help you in the future. But you also have a team that's probably stuck, or simply avoiding each other. How can the two of you facilitate dialogue with your team?

Harold: Well, first I have to say that I think this is a good beginning and I'd like to have some more of these conversations.

Art: Ditto. This is better than bickering.

Harold: I see the potential for us helping each other and the company.

Art: As for the team, I think it would go a long way with the others if they saw us as working more cooperatively. If they saw us trying to understand each other and coming up with compromises and creative solutions.

Harold: Yes. Leading by example. And I would be willing — I can't believe I'm saying this — to get the entire team together for a team dialogue. I think we could establish a different atmosphere in the team.

Art: I'm willing to have such a meeting. We could make sure everyone has a chance to say what he or she thinks. The first meeting could be focused on understanding each other better. In follow-up meetings we could use the same process to examine some of the more specific problems we face as a team.

Coach: Sounds very practical to me.

Harold: I'm much more optimistic than before.

Art: Me, too.

Harold: I have one more suggestion. Let's have the first meeting here at the beach. Art and I could facilitate a team dialogue, then we could all play golf.

Art: Half of us don't play golf, Harold. How about some body surfing instead?

Harold: Body surfing? That's for kids.

Art: No, it's not! It's a respectable sport! At least as respectable as golf!

Coach: Guys, excuse me, I have to go. Sounds like you've got plenty of material here for another dialogue.

☑ PERSONAL DEVELOPMENT SUGGESTIONS

Solicit feedback and other points of view after offering your opinion. Ask others for their reactions to something you said. For example: "Does that make sense to you?" or "Can you think of something I may have missed?" Every time you do this, you open the dialogue door a bit wider.

Avoid threatening, sarcastic, critical and close-minded comments. Certain comments are "dialogue killers." They send the message that you are not receptive to other points of view. For example: "I know what I'm talking about." Or "I can't believe you really think that." Or "You'll see I'm right." And as for sarcastic humor, you might get a laugh at the expense of cooperation.

Experiment with just asking questions during meetings. Practice drawing out others' points of view. Ask open-ended questions like "Could you help me understand why you feel that way?" or "Can you say more about that?" Avoid leading questions that start with, "Don't you think that . . . "

Solicit more active participation from the quiet folks. Some people need to be invited or encouraged to speak up in a group. (Public speaking is the number one fear in America.) As a good team leader, it is your job to draw them out in a nonthreatening way.

Say things like "I can see your wheels turning. What are you thinking?" or "You've been awfully quiet today. What do you think about what you're hearing?" or "I'd really like to know your opinion." Give them permission and a gentle push.

To gain insight, ask yourself these questions:

- Do you get defensive, frustrated or mad when people offer opinions different than yours? How do you show it? How do others react?

- Do you ask people to explain themselves? Do you try to draw them out, or do you debate their point?

Practice a mindset that will help you nurture dialogue:

- *"People are more likely to speak freely with me if I do so with them."*

- *"I learn by questioning my own assumptions."*

- *"I encourage dialogue by asking people to speak their minds."*

Chapter 7

SOLUTION-FOCUSED COACHING

"Would you please elaborate on 'then something bad happened'?"

145
What is solution-focused coaching?

Solution-focused coaching is about helping people re-move barriers to success. Between every goal and its successful achievement is a series of internal and exter-nal obstacles. Examples of internal obstacles are self-doubt, rigid thinking, and a vaguely defined objective. Examples of external obstacles include lack of support, inadequate resources and poor cooperation.

These obstacles are problems with solutions. When a team member is unable to see the solution to a problem, the whole team can get stuck. The project can get stuck. Solution-focused coaching helps teams get unstuck.

Solution-focused coaching can be outlined using the ac-ronym COACH:

Seeking	**C**larification of the situation
Understanding the	**O**bjectives of the person and team
Reviewing	**A**ctions taken so far
Generating	**C**reative options
Asking	**H**ow did we do?

Why is solution-focused coaching so important?

Teams and individuals will always encounter barriers to success. Such problems are inevitable. To help people re-move barriers, solution-focused coaching emphasizes awareness and conscious choices of what works and what doesn't work.

Another important aspect of solution-focused coaching is that it emphasizes learning. An old adage applies here: "Give someone a fish and they eat for a day. Teach them to fish and they eat for a lifetime."

Solution-focused coaching can be provided by a team leader or an outside consultant. Either way, it ultimately magnifies the capability of the team and the company. Team members learn new skills. They improve their judgment. They gain confidence as they solve challenging problems. Solution-focused coaching enhances the possibilities for creativity and customer satisfaction.

> "Good coaching is about removing barriers to success."

◈ PROFILE OF A SUCCESSFUL TEAM LEADER

Ten tips for successful solution-focused coaching:

1. **Encourage team members to think and solve problems for themselves.** The ultimate goal of coaching is to make people more accountable for their choices. When people are more confident in their own ability to solve problems, they will take more responsibility for finding and implementing solutions.

2. **Explain why a skill is important.** Research has shown over and over again that when people are told why an action is important, they show a greater willingness to do it. Knowing the importance of something stimulates people to learn more quickly and perform better.

3. **Understand that different people have different learning styles.** Of course you want to encourage people to develop new skills or think new thoughts. But keep in mind that people learn in different ways. Wise leaders coach each team member according to the individual's personality and learning style.

4. **Use patience; allow time for practice and "mind-shifting."** It takes time and repeated attempts to master a new skill. It also takes time to shift the mind to a new insight. People need the time to practice and learn from their errors if they are going to turn a new skill or a new way of thinking into a habit.

5. **Make positive comments about positive behaviors.** People need to be told when they are doing something well so they will know to continue doing it or to do more of it. Wise leaders appreciate this fact and take every opportunity to catch people doing things right.

6. **Help team members learn from setbacks.** There is no better teacher than experience and no better learning opportunity than a mistake. Effective leaders turn setbacks into learning experiences by coaching members to:
     • review what happened
     • analyze the causes
     • consider alternative choices

7. **Ask questions, use dialogue, and listen.** The purpose of a coaching session is not to assign blame for mistakes; it is to increase the individual's awareness. Good coaching involves asking the right questions to guide an individual's thinking in ways that enhance their accountability for their own actions. Good coaching involves dialogue rather than debate. And good coaching demands exquisite listening skills.

8. **Share successes and lessons learned.** Most team leaders have a wealth of experience — both successes and mistakes. When appropriate, good leaders will share their experiences with the team. They ask the team to offer their insights on why things worked or didn't work. The goal is to learn from both

success *and* failure, applying those lessons in future endeavors.

9. **Encourage and support cross-training.** The best way for team members to fully understand and appreciate each other's roles is to be able to do each other's jobs. Not only does cross-training facilitate better understanding, it also gives the team additional capability and flexibility as work requirements fluctuate.

10. **Encourage and support continuous learning and development.** Although everyone needs to be responsible for their own development, team leaders can play a significant role by helping team members plan for and get resources needed for development activities. Today's most precious resource is time, and a team leader can help make time available for members to "sharpen their saws."

⊙ DIALOGUE WITH AN EXECUTIVE COACH

" Is it time to be a superhero or a coach?"

Marsha is a team leader on the factory floor of a firm that uses just-in-time manufacturing methods. She is respected for her poise under pressure and her positive attitude. But she is frustrated with some of her team members. She believes they are too dependent on her when problems arise.

When she discovered that company executives often work with an executive coach, she asked if she could also get some help with her leadership style. They are meeting in a small office overlooking part of the manufacturing area. This is their second meeting.

Marsha: Good morning, Coach!

Coach: Hello, Marsha. You're full of energy today.

Marsha: You have to be full of energy to work here. Since we went to a just-in-time approach, we've nearly doubled our output.

Coach: That's impressive.

Marsha: Thanks. It's quite a challenge. And now they're talking about some new contracts that will double our output again.

Coach: You sound skeptical.

Marsha: Oh, I believe we can do it. My concern is that when the pressure goes up, I'll be working too many hours. I'm already putting in fifty to sixty hours a week.

Coach: Do you think the plant is understaffed?

Marsha: No. We're hiring as fast as we can. But people can't learn as fast as we need them to. Problems come up, and I end up staying late because I'm the most experienced person. We had to stop the line twice last week. That's a big deal around here. When the line stops, I don't go home until it's moving again.

Coach: We started talking about this last time. Let's go further. You mentioned that you didn't come from a manufacturing background.

Marsha: That's right. I was an emergency medical technician for five years. One of those people who arrive first at the scene of a major accident.

Coach: You were an EMT? That must have been intense work.

Marsha: It was a bit *too* intense for me.

Coach: And pretty different from this work.

Marsha: Yes and no. This is not life and death, but I use some of the same skills.

Coach: Say more about that.

Marsha: In emergency work, problems often had to be solved within seconds. A life was on the line. I learned to look at a problem, quickly make the best decision, and move forward.

Coach: Was there as much of a team approach in your other work?

Marsha: We worked in smaller teams. I always had a partner, and we often worked with police and firefighters on the scene, but it wasn't like this kind of team.

Coach: What's the difference?

Marsha: On this team it's the same group of people together for eight to ten hours. There are seven of us. It's just different.

Coach: What does it feel like to you when the line stops?

Marsha: Not quite like I'm at the scene of an accident, but I feel a sense of intense urgency.

Coach: I bet you do. Is there a lot of pressure or criticism from the executive team?

Marsha: Some, sure. There may not be a life at risk, but there's a lot of money and hassles at stake when the line stops. But I think I'm harder on myself than anybody else is.

Coach: I think that's true. Last week you said you didn't mind if I talked to some of your coworkers and other managers about your style.

Marsha: Yeah. That's totally fine with me.

Coach: So I did. And the thing I heard over and over is that whenever there's a problem on the line, everyone can depend on Marsha to solve it.

Marsha: I am a good problem solver. I'm proud of that.

Coach: "Super Marsha."

Marsha: I've heard that one.

Coach: I even heard that other teams come looking for you when there's some sort of glitch in the line. And that you're cool under pressure.

Marsha: That's me.

Coach: And everybody said they don't have to push you or worry, because you do so much of that yourself.

Marsha: They said that?

Coach: Yes. I even started wondering if some of your frustration with your team members and the other teams is misdirected.

Marsha: What do you mean?

Coach: You know the old cliché. If you give someone a fish, you feed them for a day. If you teach them to fish, you feed them for a lifetime.

Marsha: But when there's a life on the line, sometimes you just have to hand out the fish to avert a disaster.

Coach: It sounds like you approach problems at the plant like an EMT.

Marsha: I guess I do. I hate to see a problem go un-solved for very long.

Coach: And it sounds like you're so good at quickly solv-ing problems that others look to you *too* much. You end up staying late and feeling frustrated.

Marsha: I'm frustrated by the lack of responsibility. It seems like I'm the only one who jumps on problems around here. How can I get others to jump on problems so we can get the line moving again? Or prevent it from stopping in the first place?

Coach: What have you tried so far?

Marsha: I've asked for help. I've practically begged team members to get in touch with me if they can tell in advance that a problem is developing. I've voiced my frustration to the executive team, and I've asked them to provide more training to new crewmembers.

Coach: One thing I want you to know is that I, too, have recommended to the executive team that the company invest more time and money in training. I agree with you that part of this problem is the larger system you work in.

Marsha: That's good to hear. Do you think they'll do it?

Coach: I think so. They realize they have to do something. But another aspect of your frustration is more about how you lead.

Marsha: How so?

Coach: If I was trying to solve a problem and a super-hero arrived on the scene, I'd step back and defer to her superpowers.

Marsha: You're saying I'm doing too much.

Coach: Sometimes. I'm sure there are situations that call for an instant, decisive solution. That's when your crisis management skills work best. But when there's an opportunity to give someone a fishing pole, you don't take the time.

Marsha: I can see that. How do I change it?

Coach: When you approach a problem, or when someone approaches you with a problem, ask yourself which metaphor fits. Is it time to be a superhero? Or is it an opportunity to be a coach?

Marsha: I immediately go into superhero mode.

Coach: Automatically. Without asking yourself whether the situation calls for heroic superpowers or more of a mentoring kind of leadership.

Marsha: So teach me to be a coach.

Coach: I thought you'd never ask. There's a specific type of coaching I think would work for you in some situations. We call it solution-focused coaching. We train a lot of team leaders in this approach, so I carry this card that summarizes the five steps of solution-focused coaching.

Marsha: May I have a card?

Coach: Sure, you can have this one. Team leaders coach others to successful solutions by . . .

Seeking	**C**larification of the situation
Understanding the	**O**bjectives of the person and team
Reviewing	**A**ctions taken so far
Generating	**C**reative options
Asking	**H**ow did we do?

Marsha: I get it! C.O.A.C.H. It's an acronym.

Coach: Yes. It's easy to remember and helps the coach stay focused.

Marsha: I could carry this card and do a quick review before a tough meeting or a difficult conversation with a team member.

Coach: Exactly.

Marsha: But what is it you're actually trying to do as a coach?

Coach: In solution-focused coaching, I'm trying to remove obstacles that stand between the individual or the team and the solution. Another way to put it is that the coach doesn't focus as much on the problem itself as much as on the individual's approach to solving it.

Marsha: The fishing pole.

Coach: Exactly. The coach is interested in helping people learn how to solve problems — not on solving their problems for them.

Marsha: So give me the fishing pole now. Walk me through the five steps.

Coach: All right. Step 1 is to clarify the situation.

1. Clarification of the situation

Many times a problem is evading a solution because the problem is not clearly defined or understood. So I spend as much time as needed to help the person understand the problem and its context. I'll ask questions like: Who are the people involved in the problem? When did it problem start, and when does it have to be solved? What is the root cause of this problem? What will a solution look like?

Marsha: So you get the person to analyze the situation from various angles.

Coach: Whenever I can, yes. So if you were in my shoes right now, what would you be asking?

Marsha: I guess I'd want to know about a situation related to my frustration with others for not jumping in to solve problems themselves. Like when you were asking questions about whether the company is understaffed, and about how I approach crisis situations and other problems.

Coach: Right. When we were talking about that, I was trying to clarify the situation.

Marsha: So once we clarify the situation, what's next?

Coach: Then it's important to understand what's at stake, and what the people involved really want. Focusing on goals and motivation is Step 2.

2. **O**bjectives of the individual and the team

Marsha: Why not just save time and go for a solution right away?

Coach: That's the medical emergency approach and very appropriate in some crisis situations. But in many cases, the best solution depends on what the people involved really want and what purpose they feel motivated to pursue.

Marsha: In my case, I told you I want others to participate more in problem solving.

Coach: Tell me why that's important to you.

Marsha: Because I don't want to work so many hours that it messes up my family life.

Coach: Okay. Other reasons?

Marsha: I think the team would perform better, and I think they want that, too. It would free me up to focus on other improvements if I didn't have to be Super Marsha every time there's a problem.

Coach: So your personal objective is to help others become better problem solvers. You team objective is to perform better. And you're motivated by a need to keep your life in balance, take pride in your work, and because you have other areas of your work you want to improve and you need to free up time to do that.

Marsha: That says it all. And when you put it all together like that, it makes me realize how important this is to me. I really want to find a new approach to this.

Coach: That's what Step 2 is for. The coach's goal is to help the people become more aware of their own motivation.

Marsha: I can see how practical this is.

Coach: Good, let's move on to Step 3.

3. Actions taken so far

This step is about awareness and responsibility. I'm exploring what actions have been taken so far, what obstacles have emerged, and how the individual is dealing with the situation.

Marsha: Like when you were asking me how I had already tried to get my team members to depend less on me.

Coach: Precisely. The number one rule in problem solving is to do something different than you've done so far.

Marsha: So far I've either jumped on every problem myself, and felt sort of resentful and exhausted . . . or I've begged people to take more responsibility, and then it seems like they resent me, so I end up solving the problem anyway. Either way I lose.

Coach: Is it clear to you that the way you're approaching this problem is not working?

Marsha: Crystal clear. So why do I keep approaching it in a way that clearly doesn't work?

Coach: Partly because until recently I don't think you've really understood the part you play in your own problem.

Marsha: That's true. I thought of myself as a victim of other people's lack of motivation. Now I see I'm at least partly responsible for the situation because I try to be Super Marsha.

Coach: Responsibility means you have the ability to respond in another way. That's what Step 3 is based on.

Marsha: Awareness and responsibility.

Coach: But in addition to a new awareness of your responsibility in this situation, you also need to see a new *possibility*. Otherwise you'll keep spinning your wheels.

Marsha: So this leads to Step 4, right? This thing about creative options.

Coach: Yep. Once we've analyzed the situation, discovered your goal and motivation, and you've realized your portion of responsibility, we work together to generate creative options.

4. **C**reative options

Marsha: Such as this mentoring approach.

Coach: Right. But there are surely other solutions as well.

Marsha: Like additional training by the company for new staff.

Coach: That's another one.

Marsha: Or I could meet with other teams and push for additional cross-training. Then I wouldn't end up being some kind of problem solving specialist.

Coach: That's a good idea.

Marsha: Or I could request some additional compensation or time off as a reward for special skills I've contributed to the company. Maybe even a promotion.

Coach: That's another possibility. You're cookin'.

Marsha: But I think the one I really want to try at this point is solution-focused coaching. I'll think more about the other options, but I can see how this will help me in any management situation, now or in the future.

Coach: Good. Now you're ready to go out and practice the steps.

Marsha: What about Step 5?

Coach: That's for next time. I'll ask you how well this approach solved the problem. In other words . . .

    5. **H**ow did we do?

Maybe we'll talk about adjusting your approach, or maybe we'll throw it out and look for other solutions.

Marsha: The last step is about testing the first four steps and then learning from the experience.

Coach: Right. This isn't about creating some elegant theory. Successful team leadership is about making things work in the real world of teams and people. It's about solving everyday business problems. It's about reaching for peak performance by mastering skills that build on the strengths of everybody involved.

Marsha: Wow! Sounds like we're getting near the end of the book!

Coach: Just a few more pages, and then it's time to put it all to work.

☑ PERSONAL DEVELOPMENT SUGGESTIONS

Coach yourself. Create a personal development plan.
Identify one of your own barriers to success. You might pick one chapter from this book as an initial focus. Then go through the COACH model for yourself before practicing on other people. Repeat the process with other problems or obstacles. This leads to the creation of a personal development plan to guide your learning and growth.

Develop your own list of questions; think of it as a "coaching checklist." You can use the COACH model as a starting point. Refer to Appendix 2 for practical questions to employ with the COACH model. Add more questions as you think of them. Keep this checklist handy for when a coaching opportunity arises.

Make praise, reinforcement, and recognition a visible habit. When you want to encourage others, keep it simple but specific. Think of some short phrases you can tie to particular behaviors, like "I noticed how carefully you prepared that report. Well done." Such comments are a small deposit in the bank account of trust, to be drawn on later when mistakes or errors need to be reviewed.

Begin to have "lessons learned" discussions on a regular basis. Periodically ask your team, "What lessons did we learn from dealing with this customer, product, problem or situation? What worked and what didn't work? How could we do it better next time?"

Formalize the coaching process. Make coaching a formal part of your job by having coaching sessions with team members, by linking coaching sessions to performance evaluations and by encouraging everyone to make a personal development plan. You may even want to bring in professional coaches to help you get started.

Professional coaches are trained to help leaders and team members perform more effectively, improve communication skills, solve problems, make better decisions, etc. Many companies invest in their leaders by providing professional coaching as a follow-up to the 360 feedback process.

To gain insight, ask yourself these questions:

- Is anyone coaching you? If not, whom would you pick for the role? Is there a senior colleague or friend who could serve as a mentor?

- When a member of your team makes a mistake, what do you do? What could you do differently to make it an effective coaching opportunity?

Practice a mindset that will help you master solution-focused coaching:

- *"By explaining why, I empower people to perform better."*

- *"Failure is a form of feedback."*

- *"Mistakes are learning opportunities. The goal is not to make the same mistake twice."*

> "The main goal of coaching is to help people become more accountable for their choices."

Conclusion

As writers, coaches, and consultants, we are on a mission. We want to help you understand and master the skills it takes to succeed. We want you and your team to achieve peak performance.

To accomplish our mission, we have studied how people and teams grow and change. Learning new skills can require a person to change a habit or a perspective. That's not easy. In fact, most people don't change very much. Why?

Habits are stubborn creatures; some people don't change because it is hard work. Change takes fuel; some people simply don't have the motivation to keep going. Some people are mentally stuck; they suffer from hardening of the attitudes. And some people simply don't know how to change.

There are a lot of reasons.

But some people *do* change. They learn new skills to help them achieve more. You can do that. You can master these seven skills. It's totally within your power to do so.

So how *do* people change?

People who change have several things in common:
- They decide to change — one attitude, one behavior, one relationship at a time.
- They do what is doable. They don't overwhelm themselves.

- They set goals and create a plan for changing. "Here's my objective; here's how I'll get there."
- They gather support for making the change. They seek assistance from a coach, a mentor, or a buddy at work. Changers are not loners.
- They reward themselves along the way. Sometimes little rewards. Sometimes big ones. Whatever works.

You want to be one of the people who can change. You want to master new skills. That's why you picked up this book. You've already made a decision to improve.

Now you need a goal, a plan, and a starting point. If you haven't already done so, use the self-assessment in Appendix 1 as a beginning.

Rate yourself. Then ask others to give you some feedback. Compare their perceptions to your own. Remember that all feedback is valuable (even if it is not what you want to hear).

Then pick one area to work on. It might be something you've identified as needing work. It may be something your team has identified as not helpful to them. It does not have to be a big thing. Then use this book and a mentor to continue the process of mastering team leadership.

"Start now."

Appendix 1
TEAM LEADERSHIP SKILLS: SELF-ASSESSMENT

Instructions

The purpose of this assessment is for you to gain a greater awareness of your relative strengths and weaknesses as a team leader. It covers the behaviors described in the "Profile Of A Successful Team Leader" section of each chapter. These behaviors collectively make up the seven coaching skills for team leader success:

1. **L**eading by example
2. **I**nteractive listening
3. **S**timulating innovation
4. **T**rusting the team
5. **E**mpowered decision-making
6. **N**urturing dialogue
7. **S**olution-focused coaching

After you have responded to all items, compute each of the seven category scores and record them on the Team Leader Profile sheet at the end of Appendix 1.

Variations for Using This Assessment

- Complete the assessment, read the book, then complete the assessment again.
- Get team members and/or manager to assess you. Compare their assessment to yours.

1) LEADING BY EXAMPLE

1	2	3	4	5
Poor	Fair	Good	Very Good	Excellent

Score:	How well do I . . .
	1. Contribute important skills and abilities to the total team effort.
	2. Work on improving my own knowledge and skills.
	3. Display relationships skills and positive thinking.
	4. Maintain a customer focus and insist on quality.
	5. Manage time efficiently and effectively.
	6. Take initiative.
	7. Demonstrate high standards of ethical conduct.
	8. Deal fairly with people.
	9. Protect information considered by the team to be personal or confidential.
	10. Ask for support.
	= Sum of Leading by Example (out of 50)

2) INTERACTIVE LISTENING

1	2	3	4	5
Poor	Fair	Good	Very Good	Excellent

Score:	How well do I . . .
	1. Invite contact.
	2. Give my full attention to the speaker.
	3. Show a genuine interest.
	4. Listen to others without interrupting, without changing the subject, without finding fault.
	5. Maintain appropriate eye contact with the speaker.
	6. Encourage the speaker to continue talking to get more information.
	7. Notice the speaker's tone of voice, gestures and facial expressions.
	8. Ask questions to verify that I understand.
	9. Summarize the speaker's thoughts, feelings and ideas.
	10. Receive constructive feedback without getting defensive.
	= Sum of Interactive Listening (out of 50)

3) STIMULATING INNOVATION

1	2	3	4	5
Poor	Fair	Good	Very Good	Excellent

Score:	How well do I . . .
	1. Express a vision of the future.
	2. Encourage team members to ask "why" and to question the status quo.
	3. Encourage people to think creatively.
	4. Ask team members for ideas and suggestions.
	5. Suspend criticism until ideas have been heard and explored.
	6. Affirm the positive aspects of suggestions before stating my concerns.
	7. Commit time and resources to support promising new ideas.
	8. React constructively to challenges and set-backs.
	9. Give praise or recognition to team members who work on innovative projects.
	10. Live up this motto: "Never kill a new idea."
	= Sum of Stimulating Innovation (out of 50)

4) TRUSTING THE TEAM

1	2	3	4	5
Poor	Fair	Good	Very Good	Excellent

Score:	How well do I . . .
	1. Demonstrate trust by encouraging team members to work together.
	2. Put team goals above individual goals.
	3. Abide by team norms and guidelines.
	4. Interact well with different personalities of team members.
	5. Help the team address and resolve problems.
	6. Ask for team input before making hiring or assignment decisions.
	7. Support decisions made by the team.
	8. Recognize excellence and effort, and express praise.
	9. Represent the team effectively to the rest of the organization.
	10. Treat team members with courtesy and respect.
	= Sum of Trusting the Team (out of 50)

5) EMPOWERED DECISION-MAKING

1	2	3	4	5
Poor	Fair	Good	Very Good	Excellent

Score:	How well do I . . .
	1. Define the goals and explain why they are important.
	2. Solicit input from team members on decisions.
	3. "Let go" and let the team decide, when appropriate.
	4. Delegate projects and decisions based on individual strengths.
	5. Avoid making decisions for the team or for a member to whom responsibility has been assigned.
	6. Explain how much authority has been given and clearly define the boundaries.
	7. Weigh the pros and cons of several options before deciding.
	8. Take appropriate risks when necessary.
	9. Go outside the team for ideas and resources when needed.
	10. Evaluate the practicality of decisions.
	= Sum of Empowered Decision-Making (out of 50)

6) NURTURING DIALOGUE

1	2	3	4	5
Poor	Fair	Good	Very Good	Excellent

Score:	How well do I . . .
	1. State my own opinions, paying attention to tact and timing.
	2. State my opinions *clearly*.
	3. Explain the reasoning behind my opinions.
	4. Ask others for feedback and evaluation of my opinions.
	5. Communicate without ridicule or threats.
	6. Ask others for their opinions.
	7. Ask others for the reasoning behind their opinions.
	8. Demonstrate a willingness to change my mind.
	9. Avoid point-counterpoint debates.
	10. Know when to be persuasive and when to be receptive.
	= Sum of Nurturing Dialogue (out of 50)

7) SOLUTION-FOCUSED COACHING

1	2	3	4	5
Poor	Fair	Good	Very Good	Excellent

Score:	How well do I . . .
	1. Encourage team members to think and solve problems for themselves.
	2. Explain why a skill or an area of performance is important.
	3. Understand that different people have different learning styles.
	4. Practice patience with team members learning new skills and new ways of thinking.
	5. Make positive comments about positive behaviors.
	6. Help team members learn from setbacks by reviewing what happened, analyzing the causes, and considering alternative choices.
	7. Ask questions, use dialogue, and listen.
	8. Share successes and lessons learned.
	9. Encourage and support cross-training.
	10. Encourage and support continuous learning and development.
	= Sum of Solution-Focused Coaching (out of 50)

SUCCESSFUL TEAM LEADER PROFILE SHEET

Add up your scores:	
	1. **L**eading by example
	2. **I**nteractive listening
	3. **S**timulating innovation
	4. **T**rusting the team
	5. **E**mpowered decision-making
	6. **N**urturing dialogue
	7. **S**olution-focused coaching
	= Total Score (out of possible 350)

Scoring Legend:	
< 100	Uh-oh. At least you're honest. Better start reading from the beginning.
100 – 200	Still catching heat. Find the big holes and get to work.
201 – 300	Safe zone. But room to improve. Smooth out the rough edges and polish.
301 – 350	Get real. You're either (a) weak in math, (b) in love with your own image, or (c) a GREAT TEAM LEADER! To find out which is true, check your score, check the mirror, and get some 360 feedback.

Appendix 2
THE COACH MODEL

COACH spells the five steps in the solution-focused coaching cycle:

Seeking	**C**larification of the situation
Understanding the	**O**bjectives of the person and team
Reviewing	**A**ctions taken so far
Generating	**C**reative options
Asking	**H**ow did we do?

Step #1: Clarification of the situation

The first step is to clarify the situation. Before a problem can be solved, it has to be clearly defined and understood. Sometimes people focus too narrowly on the problem or rush ahead to a half-considered solution. Time spent examining the elements of a problem is well invested. The situation includes such elements as:

- Who are the people involved in the problem? Who has responsibility? Who has influence? Who, if anyone, is creating an obstacle to a solution?
- What is the nature of the problem? Is this a people problem? Is it a technical problem? Is it a financial problem? Is it a combination of these or other elements?
- When did the problem start, and when does it have to be solved? Is this a long-term problem that needs a long-term solution? Is this a crisis? Are there real deadlines, or is someone imposing

an arbitrary deadline that prevents a more thor-
ough solution?
- Where is the problem? Within the team? Between
two or more teams? Upper management? Another
geographical location?
- Why does this problem exist? What is the root
cause?

By asking these questions, you and your team members
bring focus and organization to the problem. As team
leader, you can decide to simply ask the questions and
not provide answers. Or, if the problem demands it, you
can also participate in answering the question.

Step #2: Objectives of the individual and the team

The second step of the coaching cycle is to examine the
problem in the context of an individual's and/or a team's
objectives. Every problem has more than one solution.
Every solution has to work in the context of the people
involved and the mission or the team or organization.

Questions to ask include:
- What are you and the team trying to achieve?
- How to these achievement goals influence the way
you look at the problem and its potential solutions?
- Which of the problem's potential solutions is best
for the team and its goals?
- What would be the consequences for the individual, the team, and the company if the problem
does not get solved?

- Does the problem and its solution relate to a short-term goal or part of a long-term goal?
- Why makes this problem and its solution important to you as an individual?
- How will you feel when you find a solution to this problem?
- How will you feel when the team achieves its goals?

Step #3: Actions taken so far

The third step in solution-focused coaching is to examine what efforts and methods have already been used to solve the problem. A careful analysis of actions taken so far can save time and frustration. It can also reveal partial success to build upon.

Questions to ask include:
- What have you (or we) done so far?
- What additional barriers have you run into as you try to solve this problem?
- Has anything partially helped?
- Who has been helpful in searching for a solution?
- What resources have helped most?
- What partial solution can we build upon?
- How do you feel about what you've done so far?
- What or who has been a source of support?

Step #4: Creative options

The fourth step in coaching is to create more possibilities for a solution. Creativity isn't just for artists. Business is also a creative medium, and so is problem solving.

Questions to ask include:
- What's another way we can think about this?
- Who could you talk to who has more distance from the problem?
- What options do you see?
- What options do you not see?
- What are some possible solutions you have rejected? Could an idea you've rejected be of partial value?
- What experiment could we try? Even if it is not totally successful, what could we learn that might lead to a solution?

Step #5: How did we do?

The final step in coaching is to review what the individual or team did. The goal is to learn. There will be more problems in the future. Every solution is preparation for more efficient problem solving later.

Questions to ask include:
- How did it go?
- What did you (or we) do differently?
- What worked? What didn't work?
- What did you (or we) learn from this experience?

- What type of thinking helped most in solving this problem?
- What was the most practical thing you (or we) did?
- What was the most collaborative aspect of this problem solving process?
- What could we do better next time?

Appendix 3
360 Feedback Basics

What is 360 feedback?

360 feedback is a process of getting feedback from all around you. The concept goes by a variety of other names, such as multisource feedback, peer reviews, upward feedback, multirater feedback, and more.

The various names describe the number of people in-volved (multiple sources, multiple raters) and the direc-tion of the feedback (upward or from peers). The basic idea is the same: get feedback from a variety of sources and directions. In this appendix, the term 360 feedback will be used as a general name to include all of these categories.

A new model is emerging

Traditionally, feedback has been a top-down, one-way street in organizations. Bosses give subordinates feed-back at performance appraisal sessions to explain or justify their ratings. Managers give employees feedback on how their organization is performing in sales, produc-tion, service, costs, quality, or whatever. In most cases, the majority of the feedback has been from top to bot-tom.

Many organizations are realizing that a top-down model for feedback no longer fits today's world. As companies are becoming more customer-focused, they are turning outward and soliciting more and more feedback from their customers. As companies reengineer their processes and restructure into team-based organizations, they realize that the old top-down formula no longer works when individuals are on multiple teams with different members and different leaders.

The need is growing

Depending on the organization, you may need feedback from:

- Yourself — from your own observations, perceptions and self-assessments
- Your boss — such as a supervisor, manager, or team leader
- Your subordinates — from the people working for you
- Team members — from the other members of your team, work group, or department
- Other teams — from the other groups you work with or rely on to accomplish your job (such as other shifts or other project teams)
- Customers — from the external or internal customers to whom you give your product or service
- Vendors — from the external or internal groups supplying you with resources
- Other stakeholders — from other individuals or groups who have a stake in what you do

The guiding principle

The mix of feedback and how often you get it will vary, but the principle remains the same — get continuous feedback from all around you.

In order to be responsive and adaptable in today's fast-paced, ever-changing environment, getting continuous feedback has gone from a luxury to a survival need.

Types of 360 feedback

There are a number of ways you can categorize the different types of 360 feedback:
- individual-centered feedback
- intrateam-centered feedback (within the team)
- interteam-centered feedback (between teams)
- organization-centered feedback

Individual–centered feedback

The individual is the focus and recipient of the feedback and may get feedback from managers, subordinates, and peers. This is the most common type of 360 feedback.

Typically, key managers have an individual 360 assessment done as part of their leadership development program or because their boss decides they need some improvement in their management style.

The manager fills out a questionnaire about himself/herself. The same questionnaire is then filled out by the individual's boss, subordinates, and perhaps some peers. The results are tabulated, and the manager receives a report. The manager may then review the report with others.

Based on the results, the manager may then put together an individual development plan. The plan focuses on areas needing improvement and how those improvements will be made.

Intrateam-centered feedback (within the team)

The team members are the focus of the feedback, and each member will get feedback from other team members. This type of feedback is most commonly known as peer review. It is currently the fastest growing type of 360 feedback as companies convert to team-based organizations.

Peer reviews are now being done in a variety of ways. One of the simplest forms of peer review might be called "Stop, Start, Continue." Each member of the team develops a list of items he or she will stop doing, start doing, and/or continue doing to be an effective member of the team. After reading the list to their team, the other members can confirm, modify, or suggest additions to the list. This dialogue opens the door to a wide range of reinforcing and adjusting feedback among team members.

In more structured peer reviews, the team may identify a number of dimensions or items on which they agree to be evaluated by their teammates. These items may include task-related issues like production output, quality of work, and technical skills. They may also include relationship-related issues like communication, attitude, and team management.

Team members then rate themselves and their teammates in each of the identified dimensions. They can see how their perception of themselves compares with that of their teammates. The team can then discuss their differing perceptions, giving feedback along the way.

Interteam-centered feedback (between teams)

The whole team is the focus of the feedback. They may receive feedback from other teams or groups such as management teams, steering committees, or teams they work with on a regular basis.

This type of feedback is increasing as organizations create specialty teams such as project teams, customer focus teams, and cross-functional business teams. In addition, organizations are creating team-to-team reporting relationships as they restructure into team-based arrangements (such as having work teams report to leadership teams).

An example of this type of feedback might be a project team review. Imagine a project team made up of external consultants and internal staff with the mission of developing and implementing a new company-wide information system.

The team will need feedback from a number of groups to determine if they are satisfying the needs of all the various stakeholders in terms of performance, cost, and schedule. These groups might include the user departments, the information systems group, company management, and the consulting firm management.

Organization-centered feedback

The whole organization is the focus of the feedback. It may solicit input from any individual, group, or other organization having some connection to it.

Organization-centered feedback has been in use the longest, but usually in a piecemeal fashion. Examples of organization-centered feedback include the employee opinion survey and the customer survey. In both cases, a key group of stakeholders is asked how well the organization is satisfying their needs.

An example of organization-centered feedback is the process reengineering assessment. In one version, those doing the analysis take a "horizontal picture" of the organization, following a product or process across all departments from start to finish.

They solicit feedback on how well the organization performs in terms of speed, cost, quality, and effort. They discover a wealth of new information because they look at the organization from a different angle and change the focus of the feedback to a business process.

The challenge for organizations today is to integrate these various perceptions from different points of view into a coherent, multidimensional picture of the organization. The more complex the organization, the more elaborate feedback system it needs. 360 feedback will be a key strategy for making that possible.

Applications of 360 feedback

We have looked at four different types of 360 feedback based on the focus of the recipient — the individual, the team member, the whole team, and the organization. We also saw some examples of each type.

These examples represent different applications for different purposes. Think of applications as ways the tool is applied to accomplish different objectives.

Many people think of the different applications for 360 feedback based on the objectives of the feedback or the content of the assessment. Now let's look at three common applications:

- Leadership development
- Training needs and skill assessments
- Benchmarking

Leadership development

Many larger companies today have management or leadership development programs for their middle and senior level managers. As part of these programs, a manager may be assessed by a variety of people.

The most common 360 assessment is the questionnaire in which the individual responds to a set of questions and then the individual's boss, subordinates and peers respond to the same set of questions.

The questions are usually linked to certain management and leadership behaviors that research shows are linked to high performance. Examples would include:
- Anticipates problems before they become crises
- Adapts to change in a positive manner
- Solicits a wide range of input — both facts and perceptions

Over the last twenty years, a lot of time and attention has been focused on creating "the right behavior sets." There now seems to be a general consensus about the most important competencies and skills. The most widely used 360 assessment instruments will generally cover the same territory, using slightly different words or slicing up the topics in a different way.

The basic premise behind these management programs is that good leadership skills can be learned. 360 feedback is used as an integral tool for developing the skills critical for management success.

Training needs and skills assessment

Another common application for 360 feedback is for analyzing training needs and skills in an organization. As more companies move toward continuous learning as a strategic priority, the ability to identify training needs, to develop targeted training programs, and to analyze training effectiveness is becoming increasingly important.

Soliciting 360 feedback is useful for determining:
- What training do individuals think they need?
- Is training focused on key competencies and skills?
- Is the current training sufficient and effective?
- What additional training is needed?
- Is the value received equal to the dollars invested in training?

Training-needs assessments may focus on a variety of areas, depending on the skill mix of the workforce and the complexity of the organization's planning process. They may include items like:
- company policy: understanding compensation plans
- operating systems: understanding your company's computer systems
- management skills: preparing the annual budget
- sales skills: knowing the company product line

- individual effectiveness: using time management skills to greater advantage

By using 360 feedback to assess and analyze their training needs, companies are becoming increasingly sophisticated in their ability to target the most important skills needed in the organization, and then to efficiently focus training efforts to develop those skills.

Benchmarking

As companies struggle in their journey to become world-class competitors, they need to know the answers to two important questions:

- What do our customers expect and get today?
- What are the world-class standards of performance for business cost, quality, service, lead-time, etc.?

As work groups develop in their journey to become high-performance work teams or self-managing teams, they need to know the answers to two questions:

- What do our internal customers expect and get from us?
- How do we compare to other work groups and teams in terms of performance — sales, production, quality, speed, etc.?

In both cases, the organization and the team need to solicit 360 feedback to find out how they "stack up" when compared to others like them. They need to establish benchmarks of performance so they can develop appropriate goals and set priorities.

Many companies now have benchmarking as an ongoing part of their strategic planning process. Regular and systematic studies are made of customers and competitors both inside and outside of their industry to determine what it means to be truly world-class.

Benchmarking within an organization is slowly becoming popular as companies search themselves for the "best practices" in whatever division, plant, branch, or store they may be.

Conclusion

360 feedback is an ever-expanding tool for providing improved information to organizations, teams and individuals. Designing an appropriate system takes careful planning, a lot of discussion, and a clear understanding by everyone involved.

Recommended Reading

- **On Becoming a Leader**, Warren Bennis, 1994.

- **Credibility: How Leaders Gain and Lose It, Why People Demand It**, James Kouzes and Barry Posner, 1993.

- **First, Break All the Rules: What the World's Great Managers Do Differently**, Marcus Buckingham and Curt Coffman, 1999.

- **The 21 Indispensable Qualities of a Leader: Becoming the Person Others Will Want to Follow**, John Maxwell, 1999.

- **The Magic of Dialogue**, Daniel Yankelovich, 1999.

- **Managers as Mentors**, Chip Bell, 1996.

- **Masterful Coaching**, Robert Hargrove, 1995.

- **Masterful Coaching Fieldbook**, Robert Hargrove, 1999.

- **Organizing Genius: The Secrets of Creative Collaboration**, Warren Bennis and Patricia Ward Biederman, 1998.

A portion of the profits from the sale of this book will go to Children, Inc.

Through Children, Inc. individuals and organizations can sponsor children around the world to help fund basic necessities.

For more information about how to sponsor a child, write or call:

Children, Inc.
1000 Westover Road
P.O. Box 5381
Richmond, Virginia 23220
1-800-538-5381

Meet the Writing Team

MARK KELLY is a management consultant and senior management team coach. He is a partner at Raleigh Consulting Group, Inc. Mark also wrote *The Adventures of a Self-Managing Team* and *The TeamTraining Manual.* Contact him at Kelly@RaleighConsulting.com.

ROBERT FERGUSON, PHD, is an executive coach, a professional speaker, and an associate at Raleigh Consulting Group, Inc. He is also a psychologist in private practice with Main Street Clinical Associates in Durham, NC. Contact him at Robert.Ferguson@Mindspring.com.

GEORGE ALWON is a management consultant and executive coach. He is the managing partner at Raleigh Consulting Group, Inc. RCG has been helping companies navigate change since 1979. Contact him at Alwon@RaleighConsulting.com.

Resources

Books: Visit our website at www.RaleighConsulting.com to order books. Or go to Amazon.com. For quantity discounts or to inquire about special arrangements, call Mark Kelly at 800-825-4306.

360 Feedback: Parts of this book were adapted from 20/20 Insight GOLD, an award-winning 360 feedback program from Performance Support Systems, Inc. To see a demonstration of this powerful software system, go to their web site at www.2020insight.net.

Executive Coaching: Contact an author directly, or visit Raleigh Consulting Group's web site:

www.RaleighConsulting.com

Speaking, Consulting, and Training: Raleigh Consulting Group offers a variety of talks, training events, and consulting services. For more information, go to our web site or call Mark Kelly at 800-825-4306.

"Good coaching is about remov-
ing barriers to success."